The Technique of Filet Lace

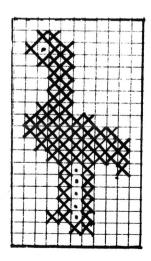

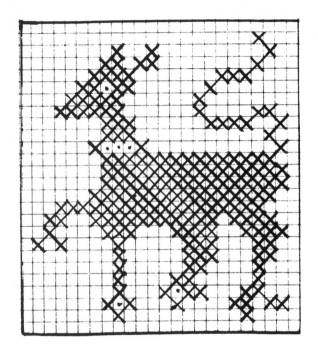

The Technique of Filet Lace

Pauline Knight

B T BATSFORD LIMITED, LONDON

© Pauline Knight, BA, 1980
First published 1980
ISBN 0 7134 1698

Filmset by Willmer Brothers Limited
Birkenhead, Merseyside
Printed in Great Britain by
The Anchor Press Ltd
Tiptree, Essex
for the publishers B T Batsford Limited
4 Fitzhardinge Street London W1H 0AH

Contents

Acknowledgment

It is a pleasure to acknowledge the encouragement and inspiration given to me by Mrs Dorothea Nield of the Embroiderers' Guild, without whom this book would not have been prepared.

To Mrs Enid Purvis I would express my thanks and appreciation of her kindness in lending many examples of Lacis from her collection, for me to examine and have photographed. To Mrs Hall is owed the pleasure of the use of the bedspread worked by her grandmother and aunt.

My gratitude is due to Miss S M Levey, Assistant Keeper of the Textile Department of the Victoria and Albert Museum, for her detailed replies to my queries, and also to her assistant, Miss Fox-Robinson, who patiently helped me to examine so many examples of Lacis in the Museum. My thanks are due to my local photographer at Studio Heather for his patience with unusual work, and to Donald Hanley for his enlargements. I am also grateful to Mrs Joyce Long who typed the manuscript and to Mrs Dorothy Cox for her help in proof reading.

PK
Bexhill on Sea, 1980

Introduction

The formation and rapid development of the Lace Guild is an indication of the revival of interest in this craft. Both day and residential courses in lacemaking are in demand. Old books are reprinted and new publications issued, concentrating chiefly on bobbin lace, some of the attraction being the bobbins themselves and the search to possess old ones.

Less well-known is the kind often called *filet lace*, though historically better known as *lacis*. (Both names are French and deserve to be given their French pronunciation). It may be because the name *filet crochet* (that strange contradiction of terms) is familiar to us that we have not adopted the old name. Both will be used in the text, *filet* more frequently for the work of recent years, when it was popular around the turn of the century.

The earlier history of lacis is connected with its use in the churches, on altar linen and furnishings and for embellishing the special vestments worn by the priests. It was also a favourite occupation in Continental courts and the houses of the nobility, especially in France and Italy. It continued to be made in the convents, and, until quite recently, was taught as part of the education of 'young ladies' at Swiss and French 'finishing schools'.

It deserves to become popular again, being in many ways simpler than bobbin laces, less expensive in outlay, more convenient to handle and carry around and having a variety of practical uses in the home. The tools needed are few: in fact those in the active needlewoman's basket *could* suffice. For it is merely a matter of darning designs on a prepared hand-made net. Because such net is not now readily available it means making the net oneself first and so delaying the pleasure of producing a piece of lace. Yet netting is, in itself, an old lace craft, deserving to be acknowledged as such and to be learnt for its own sake.

A variety of threads can be used, whether for fine work or bolder effects and thus it will appeal to different tastes and ages of workers who will be able to produce articles from pincushion size to that of curtains. There are fascinating traditional designs to copy, dating from the sixteenth century onwards, with formal geometric or floral patterns, heraldic 'beasties', and whole scenes from fables and myths. There is also the possibility of creating original designs to suit modern trends and ideas.

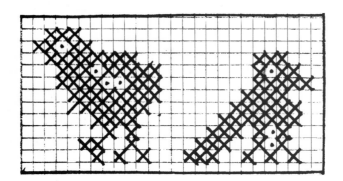

Historical Background

Filet lace is often connected with the crochet patterns which have been copied or adapted from lacis. Sixty years ago this type of crochet was worked by young ladies, before their marriage, to edge large table cloths, and for tray cloths and d'oyleys. Not only ladies of the leisured classes were thus occupied: it was also a common activity during the lunch breaks in offices, shops and factories. Younger girls were taught to crochet and designs were exchanged.

Earlier in the century and in the late nineteenth century more ambitious needlewomen made filet using hand-made knotted net bought from the Continent. With a few English journals, publishing instructions and designs there appeared advertisements by people prepared to make the linen net. In the *Needlecraft Monthly Magazine* of May 1908 'Filet Squares of 48, in linen thread. 7s 6d dozen. Squares of 25, 3s 6d dozen.' were advertised.

In the same volume, for January, there was a most interesting article about the work of Lady Viola Talbot, daughter of the Earl of Shrewsbury. There are two illustrations of squares of filet joined by embroiderie Anglaise, for a cot cover and for a bedspread. The cot designs include a unicorn with other animals, while the bedspread has figures that date from much earlier centuries. Amazingly Lady Viola intended to copy the famous Bayeux Tapestry in filet

lace. With special permission a copy was made, on the understanding that the designs were to be carefully guarded and not given to anyone else. A Paris firm had undertaken to reduce the tapestry designs to a size suitable for reproduction in filet work.

Lady Viola believed it would take five years for her to copy the tapestry. Though the Royal School of Needlework has produced an embroidered copy, now seen in a special 'dome' in Hastings, I have found no reference to one in filet. If anyone feels moved to undertake the task, the earlier part of the designs *were* published in a French album, in my possession: unhappily I see no possibility of carrying out the work myself.

Only a few English needlework magazines published articles on netting and filet lace. It was the French albums that provided a rich store of designs, reproducing some of the old sixteenth and seventeenth century ones, with others specially designed of a similar type. It would not now be possible to distinguish originals from imitations. A description given of the designs in one album includes styles: Arabe, Egyptien, ancien, Gothique, Persan, Japonais, Renaissance Italienne, Louis XVI, Empire, with also motifs from the Fables of La Fontaine and the Tales of Perrault. Many such albums were published and can be found by the diligent searcher.

They are the source of many of the designs illustrated in this publication.

For so many books of designs to be published there must have been numerous purchasers making the lace themselves or employing others to make it for them. An intriguing example is seen in the round cloth (figure 1) made as a wedding present, not, I should think, by one person. The complete design, given in one book, has been marked (by its previous owners) as 'Empire' with the number of meshes (455 × 455).

1 Circular cloth in linen (toile) stitch made in France as a wedding gift, nineteenth century. It shows emblems and figures representing the various cantons (Mrs Purvis's Collection)

In a different book are two winged figures, almost identical with the four at the central points of the inner part (figure 2); while the four strange chimera and the dolphins appear also elsewhere, as do the two soldier-like heads and the charming lady ones. All are set within beautiful traceries of leaf designs.

The large bedspread (figure 3) is an excellent example of the gathering together of designs from different publications, and combining them with squares of embroidered linen. Two corner squares of lacis show a unicorn and a heraldic lion, while a burdened elephant and a fierce-looking Jove fill the other two corners. Most of the other lacis squares depict scenes from La

Fontaine or Perrault (figures 4a, b, c) with another of a most realistic fisherman. Whether these actually had been designed and worked at the time that the fables were written ie during the reign of Louis XIV, the Sun King, (1643–1715), I am very doubtful.

The central square of Charité is similar to the figures of Prudence and Justice which are in the same volume as the heraldic eagle and the two people, who are named in my copy as Louis XV and Marie Leizinsha (figure 6) – the eagles and fleur-de-lis give the arms of France and Austria. Those who completed the bedspread must have looked elsewhere for the winged serpent.

From another book of designs it can be seen how those who used them adapted them for their special purpose. It is probable that the piece of lacis (figure 7) was made in the early twentieth century but the significance of the bull's head and four fishes is not known, though clearly suggesting it formed a nobleman's badge. In the printed design the fruit being piled, rather precariously, by the kneeling figures into each opening of the cornucopias is repeated, more carefully poised, on vases beside the figures. This must have made for a wider piece than was intended so that vases were omitted. The enlarged photograph of a kneeling figure (figure 8) reveals the details of the stitchery, all in toile.

To be able to appreciate the working out of the elaborate design of the large French cloth (figure 9) a corner has been enlarged (figure 10). Linen stitch is used throughout, yet a clever use of a white linen thread on the dark thread of the fine net ground with a few dark leaves gives contrasting light and shade, while the dark curving band unites leaves, fruits and flowers.

Variety obtained by a different method is seen in the small portion of

2 *Winged figures from a design book – the figures are similar to those in figure 1*

the tablecloth worked by Mrs Purvis when a young learner of the lace (figure 11). The dolphins are worked in toile, while for the central square and its corners the reprise stitch is worked in a heavier thread.

It will be noticed that in most of the pieces examined there are the two stitches used, with the toile predominating. Quite different is the cloth of filet squares joined by tatting (figure 12).

(a)

(b)

*3 Bedspread of embroiderie Anglaise
with filet (lacis) squares depicting scenes
from fables (Mrs Purvis's Collection)*

*4 Details of three scenes from the beds-
pread
a The fox and the crow
b Red Riding Hood
c A man fishing*

(c)

5 *Centre of the bedspread – Charité*
(Mrs Purvis's Collection)

6 *Louis XV and Queen, heraldic eagle*
(Mrs Purvis's Collection)

Here are elaborate designs using a variety of embroidery stitches with, it seems, no intention of reproducing simple filet lace. This, and the border of the altar cloth may perhaps be of the late eighteenth or the nineteenth century. The latter has a background of square net mostly covered with lace stitch, and spaces of plain net are left behind the I H S and the heart. An embroidery stitch, (sometimes described as reprise and used for narrow leaves) here composes the many petalled flowers.

Perhaps it is here that reference should be made to Madame Goubard's *Book of Guipure D'Art*[1] published in 1869. It was offered as 'an imitation of the celebrated ancient Guipure lace', described as having been made of thin vellum covered with gold, siver or silk thread. Embroidery stitches included the point de toile and point de reprise with point d'esprit, point de feston, point de Bruxelles and wheels and stars. Those needlewomen acquainted with the DMC *Encyclopedia of Needlework*[2] will recognise that these are some of the stitches given there to be worked on filet net to produce filet brodé, filet guipure, Cluny guipure and Richelieu guipure.

The good condition of the length of lace shown in figure 13 suggests that it belongs to the nineteenth century or early twentieth century, although the design is more compact and complicated than was general at this time. The birds in figure 14 may be an

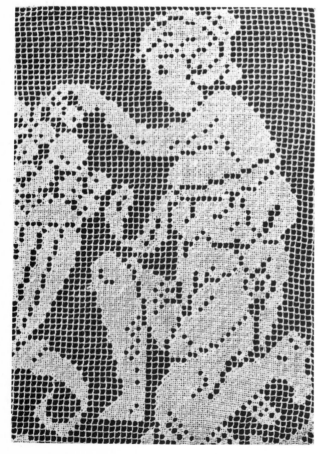

7 Early twentieth-century filet lace showing coronet and crest, four fishes in a laurel wreath and a bull's head below, cornucopia and kneeling figures (Mrs Purvis's Collection)

8 Enlargement of one of the kneeling figures

9 Nineteenth-century French tablecloth on fine dark net with linen stitch in fine and heavy threads giving a variety of textures (Mrs Purvis's Collection)

10 Detail of corner of tablecloth (Mrs Purvis's Collection)

older piece. They are less firmly darned than the two deer running towards the formal centre design (figure 15). This is firmly and correctly worked from an old design, though its date is doubtful. Somewhat similar is the triangle with the two facing sea horses (figure 16).

Another piece which may be a reproduction of an old design and does suggest, possibly, the eighteenth century, has the peculiar flower between the floral medallions, themselves encircled within groups of leaves (figure 17).

The unusual design shown in figure 18, said to be Dutch, but not definitely date-fixed, is worked diagonally on the net. It is interesting to examine the different effects provided for the centres of the tulips, surrounded by the darning and with the flower outlined in a slightly heavier thread. The leaf shapes which arcade each flower are most unusual: the treatment of the vandyke edge lightens the whole design.

The lace so far described and illustrated, mostly of the twentieth and late nineteenth centuries, will give some idea of the enthusiasm of this revival of interest in filet.

This revival had been preceded by a period from which there is little evidence of this form of lace being produced. The reason? Probably the invention of lace machines and the development of the Nottingham lace industry providing bedspreads and long curtains in elaborate designs, very cheaply.

Women were no less busy with their

11 Circular tablecloth on knotted mesh, with toile and reprise stitches, depicting dolphins (Mrs Purvis's Collection)

12 Part of a nineteenth-century altar cloth. The lace squares are embroidered with various stitches and joined with tatting (Mrs Purvis's Collection)

13 Nineteenth-century piece with central
octagonal design and surrounding circle
and festoons, toile stitch is used

14 Probably eighteenth- or nineteenth-
century lace edging showing two birds
either side of flower design, toile stitch is
used

15 *Two running stags facing; eighteenth
or nineteenth century?*

16 *Triangle with two mythical fish-tailed
horses facing; nineteenth century?
(Mrs Purvis's Collection)*

17 *Lacis on square knotted mesh depicting
unusual flower between floral
medallions; eighteenth century?*

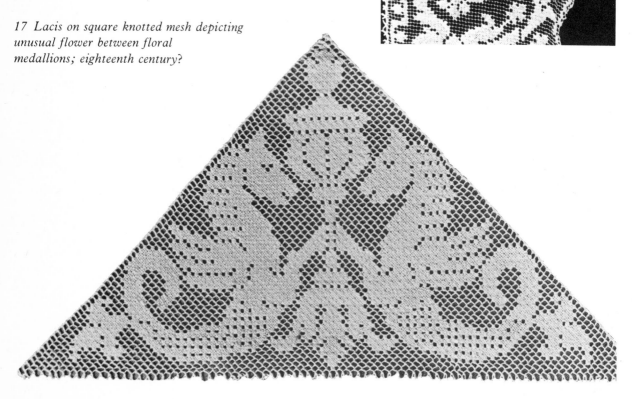

needles. In England in the eighteenth century, quilts, hangings, curtains, fire-screens and even embroidered carpets occupied their leisure. An interesting account by an Embroiderers' Guild member,[3] in *Embroidery* for 1961, describes how in the Royal Palace in Madrid she was fascinated by the Gasparini room from the late eighteenth century. For while the artist was painting the ceiling he also provided the designs for the embroiderers to adapt to wall panellings and furniture coverings. This gives a definite example of the cooperation, on site, between designers and needlewomen which had been customary for many years previously.

I imagine there must have been some such preparation for the impressive hanging, only parts of which can be illustrated (figure 19). It consists of 127 oblongs of cut work, 72 squares of reticella and 56 squares of lacis. The latter is of a different variety from that earlier described. Flowers and leaves in conventional shapes of an amazing variety, usually spreading from a central vase form, are outlined by the heavier thread which joins them within the square design. A study of the piece and

of the enlargements (preferably with a magnifying glass) reveals that almost every square is different, yet there is a similarity in the development of the basic shape. The designer certainly had an ingeniously delightful task in preparation and the lacemakers must have had great skill and patience to complete the work. It is dated 1620 which will account for the name since given to this kind of lace – Filet Richelieu – in compliment to Cardinal Richelieu, so important in France during the reign of Henry IV. Yet the work is described as Italian. It continued to be popular and was reproduced in the D M C publications as a form of filet brodé in the nineteenth century period. Another simple design worked by this method is seen in figure 22.

Journeying backward in time to earlier lacemaking brings us to the seventeenth and sixteenth centuries from which we still have much lacis available

18 Unusual vandyked edging on knotted net worked diagonally with floral shapes in linen and reprise stitch, possibly Dutch (*Mrs Nancy Evans, International Old Lacers, USA*)

in the Victoria and Albert Museum in London. We think mostly of lacis as worked with white linen threads and applied to linen. Yet at this time coloured silk threads were often used for the fine netting with white linen thread for the reprise stitchery. Or, in reverse, the ground has been netted in a natural thread and various colours used for the design. References to this coloured work trace it chiefly to Italy and Sardinia. A variation admired by 'Carita'[4] was a hanging in the hall of Sir John Foskowe, in Henry VIII's time, of green silk bordered with 'darning'. The combination of green silk with bands and squares of lacis apparently was popular for some years.

19 Hanging of large filet squares and oblongs of linen with needlepoint and reticella. Richelieu style, 1620 (Mrs Purvis's Collection)

Photographs in the Victoria and Albert drawer describe an early Italian piece worked with white linen thread on a yellow silk canvas. The border contained figures offering a sacrifice; they were outlined in red silk.

Perhaps such ideas of using colours will inspire modern lace workers to experiment? Where I have done so, the black and white photographs will only partly convey the effect, as in the mat with the lily-of-the-valley design (figure 23).

The most favoured design on bands and borders of lacis for many years was the vine, sometimes simply the leaves in a counter-change arrangement, but more often including the grapes and tendrils, often fancifully portrayed. There is a similarity in the borders (figure 24) which may be Italian or German. They share an elaboration of design and technique, with a heavier

20 Detail of three squares of the hanging   21 Larger detail of one square

22 *Square in Richelieu style*
(Mrs Purvis's Collection)

23 *Circular mat with lily-of-the-valley*
design worked in green and white no. 20
crochet thread (diameter 22 cm − 8½ in.)

24 *Italian or German lacis on knotted*
square netting with birds reaching up to
central tree

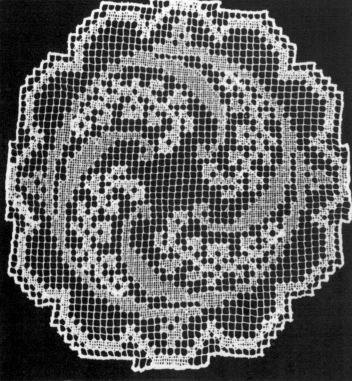

thread edging part of the curving stems and outlining the leaves and the two unusual flowers with their rather puzzling lines of dots and small circles which form the flower centres. One includes two birds with wings fully outspread, stretching to touch the tips of the strange flowering plant placed conventionally between them. They appear alternately at the top and the base of the border as the curve reaches its other edge (figure 25).

There is a study in contrasts in the treatment of the vine leaves in the two designs from the Victoria and Albert Museum records, both Italian of the sixteenth century, as also in the form of arcading. The leaves in the first band are worked solidly in toile as are the grapes and the interlacings of the separating chain. Yet there is a lightening of the whole appearance by the small pointed shapes running along all the edges of chain and leaf stalks (figure 26).

About the second border the caption states 'the pattern is in white thread and consists of a conventional vine-stem from which spring leaves, bunches of grapes and tendrils. Small birds are pecking at the fruit.' On the border the leaves give interesting examples of how the two stitches, toile and reprise, were used with also a darker and a lighter thread in breaking up the solidity of the leaf. To me the result is somewhat

25 Lacis – linen stitch is in finer thread, reprise (darning stitch) is in a heavier thread. Date of work is 1878 possibly of German origin

26 Border of square mesh lacis showing conventional vine stem, sixteenth century (Victoria and Albert Museum, ref. 22802, London)

shaggy, though I admire the way in which the almost separated leaves shape to gently curving points. On a square mesh that is not as simple as it may appear (figure 27).

To examine this technique more closely an enlargement is given in figure 28(b) of part of the border in figure 28(a). This close-up may not reveal the graceful leaf which results and perhaps the one worked separately (figure 29) may persuade someone to try it out, even including the scroll-tipped extensions to leaf-points. Here is another method of filling spaces yet lightening the design, which also recalls similar shapings on some illuminated manuscripts.

Notice how the small designs of the borders also use both stitches: this could give the worker practice in neatly and unobtrusively passing the thread along correctly. Only a small portion of the lattice effect pattern is seen but perhaps enough to indicate how the darning is worked diagonally across the squares.

The conventional 'flower-pot' design appears in figure 30 between the two seated lions, the curvings of whose long tails nicely fill the spaces above them. Here the enlargement (figure 31) shows that the heavy lines and outlining squares are worked in reprise. But for the mass of their bodies the embroidery stitch (called point d'esprit, or loop, or lace stitch) is used and coloured threads, now faded, for various diamond shapes breaking its monotony. This unusual treatment cleverly suggests their manes, and the whole gives a realistic picture of the animals. It was probably Venetian work of the sixteenth century. Another interesting example is that of the Unicorn design shown in figure 32.

Not *all* lacemakers of that period were so ambitious or were employed to

27 Band of lacis with vine and grape design and small birds pecking at fruit (Victoria and Albert Museum, ref. 22802, London)

*28(a) Border of Italian lacis, possibly
Sardinian seventeenth-century work; toile
and reprise stitches used
(Mrs Purvis's Collection)*

*28(b) Enlargement of part of the border
shown in figure 28(a)*

*29 Leaf from the border worked sep-
arately to show toile and reprise stitches
used*

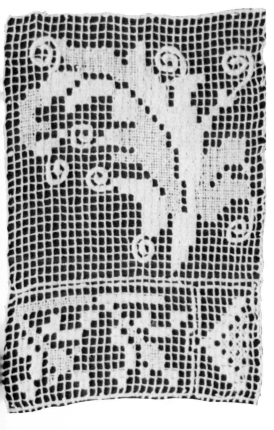

make spectacular specimens. More
homely, useful articles were also produced. So three are shown (figures 33,
34, 35) also of the sixteenth century
which could give pleasure to anyone
now to make.

Although it was not darned on a
square net ground but on a canvas or
on loosely woven linen gauze material,
the designs and methods of working of
what is known as buratto lace are normally included with lacis. In figure 36
there will again be seen the peculiar
scroll extensions to leaves; the lower

30 *Lacis, Italian (Venetian?), sixteenth century showing two lions and the much used conventional 'flower-pot' design (Mrs Purvis's Collection)*

31 *Enlargement of one of the lions showing toile, reprise and lace stitches*

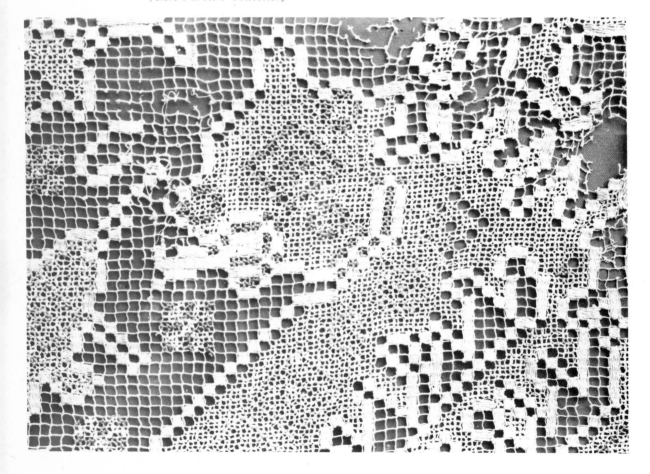

32 Lacis edging, Italian, sixteenth century
(Collection of Jules and Kaethe Kliot)

33 Circular mat with four eight-petalled flower shapes and stepped buttonhole edge, from a sixteenth-century design

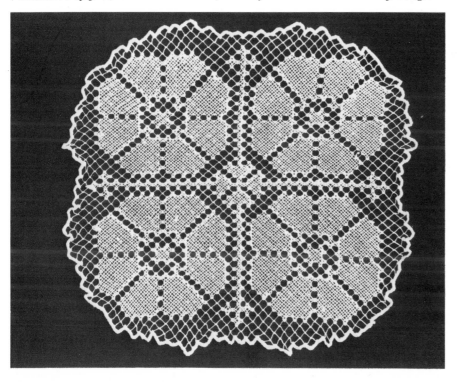

34 Octagonal mat with central diamond and petal-shaped designs at corners and stepped buttonhole edge, from a sixteenth-century German design. The diagram shows the working of the mat

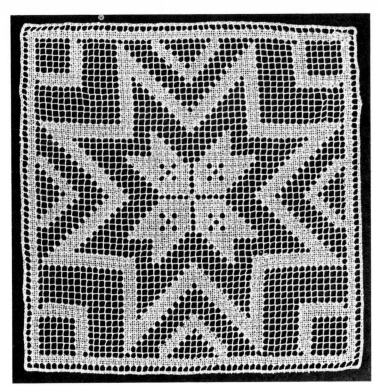

35 *Square mat with eight-pointed star design worked with green crochet thread on white net, from a sixteenth-century German design. The mat is 18 cm (7 in.) square. The diagram shows how the mat is worked*

lace-edged design on figure 37 was probably Sicilian buratto work of the late sixteenth century and gives a formal geometric effect to less obvious leaf patterns.

The design shown in figure 38 seems to have no reference to definite leaves or flowers though vaguely suggesting growing forms, again with the scroll-edged extensions: this was worked on canvas, again Sicilian buratto work. Below it is seen a late sixteenth-century piece of lacis – a vine design in counterchange (figure 39).

In the section of the buratto altar cloth (figure 40) and the enlargement, the stitch can be seen as reprise throughout. That is true also of the earlier, more spectacular piece which is Italian of the fifteenth century, giving an exciting scene of soldiers with dogs (figure 42). Yet again we see the central vaguely tree-like shape between two facing dogs.

One of the most attractive pieces of lacis illustrated is that showing the Spanish grandees and their ladies (figures 43, 44). This late sixteenth-

36 Early sixteenth-century Sicilian buratto lace (Mrs Purvis's Collection)

37 Buratto lace, possibly Sicilian, from a late sixteenth-century lace album

38 Buratto lace darning on canvas, possibly Sicilian, from a lace album

39 Lacis with linen stitch showing vine design in counterchange, possibly Italian of the late sixteenth-century from Frederick Fischbach's Lace Album Designs for Lace, *1878*

century piece of lacis is in good condition and carefully preserved in the Victoria and Albert Museum, while postcards are available on the display shelves. I was permitted to examine it closely: the enlargement of one figure of the photograph (figure 45) helps us to see how simple varieties of a few stitches have given the effect of different substances, while there are delightful lacy patterns for the ladies' garments. An uneven thickness of the thread makes a rough surface on the linen stitch for the horses, the man's face, and bird's wing. A heavier couched thread gives a firm outlining to the main figures, and continues to pass round the squares of the net to suggest ruffs at the neck and waved hair for the ladies. Variations of straight and diagonal lines suggest for the latter two fashion styles for their dresses. Squares of toile alternating with 'spiders' adorn the centre of the lady riding pillion, whose elaborate hair-do may mean that she is of greater dignity than the

two with the small hats and feather cockades. There are many variations of small blocks of reprise and spaces filled with wavy lines or circles or stars. The Don's jabot has large star effects, each covering squares of four meshes, down each side of the central line of stitchery. The small heraldic lions marching round between candelabra and tree forms, the birds, trees and flowers all complete a delightful picture which could provide a wealth of designing ideas for lacis.

The Seven Centuries of Lace[5] is the most comprehensive book I have seen illustrating lace. The author, Mrs Hungerford Pollen, had examined some early work in Italy (eg the 'Assisi' and 'Boniface' albs). She gives a careful analysis of the historical evidence available about early lace and a detailed account of all the stitches, with their Italian names. Queries have since been raised about the dating given to the early examples, which she had named as fifteenth-century work. However, as

*40 Buratto lace altar cloth, sixteenth-
century Italian (possibly Sicilian). The
mesh is hand woven with a needle and
thread on a frame and afterwards the
pattern is made with darning stitch on the
meshes (Mrs Purvis's Collection)*

41 Enlargement of part of the altar cloth

*42 Border of lacis with twisted mesh
called buratto. The design is Italian possibly of the fifteenth-century and is worked in* punto a rammendo *showing numerous armed men and animals (152 cm
long × 23 cm wide—5 ft × 9 in.). Plate
XVII from Mrs Hungerford Pollen's*
Seven Centuries of Lace, *1908*

photographs in the Victoria and Albert
Museum give those dates, it is possible
that she repeated them in her book.
Experts now believe that the sixteenth
century is the earliest period to which
one can definitely assign the lace that
has survived.

Figures 46–52 are of plates taken
from her book and illustrate the repetition of designs used in filet lace
from century to century and between
different countries.

The inscription on her Plate XI
(figure 46) has found no interpreter, it
appears, nor is there knowledge about

the 'R', so these can give us no clue to
the date. The whole design is clearly of
religious significance. 'The glory of
flames' surrounding the I H S has the
same suggestion of radiating power, in
the alternate waved and straight lines
which will be seen surrounding the
circle of the dove at the centre of the
neck of an alb, illustrated in her book as
Plate XXXVII. The same effect, we
note, was used on the chalice veil, of
French work of 1668, seen in *The Art
of Embroidery*[6] plate 372. The little 'angular angels' at the ends of some rays
are unique and the peacock is more
sharply clawed than is usual, with a
strange head-erection. The introduction
of tiny crosses around the body of the
peacock would relate to ecclesiastical
work. One also notices here the reluct-
ance of early designers to leave any
empty spaces, but to use stars, trees or
odd birds to fill them.

The caption to Plate XII (figure 47)

43 *Part of band of lacis (134 cm long*
×64 cm wide – 7 ft 8½ in. ×2 ft 1 in.).
Spanish from second half of the sixteenth
century (Victoria and Albert Museum,
ref. 70719 1207, London)

44 *Another part of the band (Victoria*
and Albert Museum, ref. 70720 1207,
London)
45 *Enlargement of one figure from the*
band

46 Border of lacis in punto a tela *or linen stitch with religious inscriptions: a fanciful peacock and the letters I H S surrounded by a glory of flames and by little angular angels. Italian of late sixteenth-seventeenth century (147 cm long × 86 cm wide—4 ft 10 in. × 2 ft 10in.). Plate XI from Mrs Hungerford Pollen's* Seven Centuries of Lace, *1908*

gives details of this altar cloth which the author suggested 'may possibly have been made for Richard II, as his two wives were both French and this piece has the stag, which was the royal device'. The I H S is repeated in different surrounding designs in two of the hexagonal divisions shown. The chain kind of interlacing occurs also in the vine border examined earlier (figure 26), while the two heraldic lions are the exact images of those seen in the Spanish picture. As we have realised, there was no restriction on design copying, between countries, in later years, or even centuries. 'Carita' showed them in her book from which was made my copy (figure 114).

The rather heavy design of the lacis squares in the part of a quilt (figure 48) while suggesting floral shapes yet has a geometric formality, definitely seen in the enlarged square (figure 49). They would probably be described as 'Gothic'.

47 Border of square mesh lacis intended probably for an altar cloth with a design of ornamental hexagonal compartments worked in linen stitch in each of which were various devices: I H S in a heart-shape above two heraldic lions, a stag, pairs of birds, symmetrical devices of leaf and blossom (182 cm long × 25 cm wide– 6 ft × 10 in.). The border is French of the late sixteenth/early seventeenth centuries. Plate XII from Mrs Hungerford Pollen's Seven Centuries of Lace, 1908

The lower square of her Plate XVI (figure 50) corresponds in style with the hanging already examined, of 1620, where leaves and grapes are outlined in heavier thread, the style persisting for many years as Filet Richelieu. On the Vandyke Border above it will be noticed that the cut edges of the net are not buttonholed: that was a later development. As it is named English work of the sixteenth century the Tudor Rose was most probably intended to be represented (figure 51).

If one were able to examine the full 1·68 m (5 ft 6 in.) of the lacis table cover – her Plate XVI (figure 52) it

would be seen as much lighter in design than most we have so far dealt with. The heraldic 'Lion Rampant' in the cartouche suggests that it was made for a wealthy nobleman, as does the use of gold thread to outline and enrich the design and the bobbin-made lace for the edging. One cannot decide what flowers were intended.

A number of actual examples of lacis have now been examined and others appear on later pages. Further discussion of its history must be obtained from books, where there are repetitions of the same facts and ideas.

But first let us turn to the books from which designs were obtained for the lace. The earliest dates are, in Cologne 1527, in Venice about buratto lace 1559, by Federico Vinciolo 1587, then in Italy by Elisabeth Catanea Parasole 1597, and in France by Matthias Mignerack 1605. English ladies had to wait until 1632 for *A Scholehouse for the Needle* by Richard Shoreleyker. In the Introduction he writes:

> *Here Followeth*
> *Certaine Patternes*
> *Of Cut-workes: and but once Printed*
> *before.*

Also sundry sorts of Spots, as Flowers, Birds and Fishes and will fitly serve to be wrought, Some with Gould, some with Silke, and some with Crewell, or otherwise at your pleasure.

> *London. Printed in Shoe-Lane, at The Signe of the Faulcan, by Richard Shoreleyker 1632*

My interest in examining the facsimile in the Victoria and Albert Museum of Shoreleyker's book was in the designs given, especially the early interlacing patterns, the swastikas, the fleur-de-lis, and many flowers and birds including the phoenix and pelican. Neither in this

48 *Part of a quilt made of squares of lacis work with oblongs of linen in which are squares worked in needlepoint called reticello or cutwork (111 cm long × 71 cm wide – 3 ft 8 in. × 2 ft 4 in.). The quilt is* *Italian of the seventeenth century. Plate XIV from Mrs Hungerford Pollen's* Seven Centuries of Lace, *1908*

49 *Enlargement of one square*

nor any of the other books were any instructions given. Clearly, therefore, the needlewomen were previously well-skilled and could apply the patterns to their type of work. Richard Shoreleyker tried to be specially helpful with these concluding words:

> I would have you knowe, that the use of these squares doth showe, how you may contrive any worke, Bird, Beast or Flower, into bigger or lesser proportion, according as you shall see cause: As thus if you will enlarge your patterne, devide it into squares: then rule a paper as large as ye list into what squares you will: then looke how many holes your patterne doth containe. Upon so many holes of your ruled paper drawe your patterne.

He even provided a page with squares of two different sizes.

In the book by Elisabeth Parasole some of the designs were on square net, but the majority were for reticella or for *punto in aria.*

These books and others later were often reprinted. The one which was the most popular and plagiarised later, we now have available in a facsimile edition, with translations into English of

interesting dedicatory prefaces. It is the one by Federico Vinciolo.[7] On pages 45 to 92 there are designs for lacis, most of them blocked out on a square mesh and many even giving the number of meshes needed for the designs. This was the source for many of the patterns in nineteenth-century books.

Among those who made use of Vinciolo's book was Catherine de Medici. In her book Mrs Palliser[8] reports that her servants made so many squares of netting that 381 were found

50 Part of a quilt of squares of lacis; the one shown has the pattern of a vine alternating with rectangles of linen decorated with small cutwork (99 cm long × 60 cm wide – 3 ft 3 in. × 2 ft.) The work is German, sixteenth century. Plate XVI (2) from Mrs Hungerford Pollen's Seven Centuries of Lace, *1908*

51 Vandyke border of knotted square mesh darned in linen stitch with repeated large and small blossoms; the larger ones resemble Tudor roses (122 cm – 4 ft long). The border is English of the sixteenth century. The pattern in both figures 51 and 52 is outlined and partly worked with punto riccio. *Plate XVI from Mrs Hungerford Pollen's* Seven Centuries of Lace, *1908*

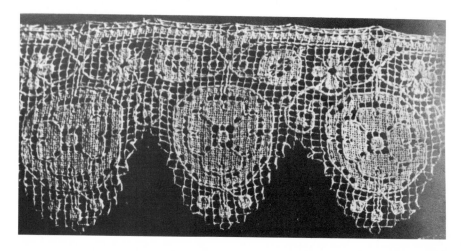

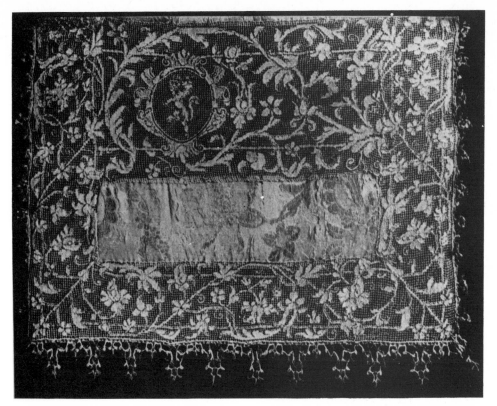

52 *Lacis table cover of square mesh net worked in linen stitch with scrolls, leaves etc, amidst which are cartouches of foliated shields bearing a heraldic lion in the centre. The pattern is outlined and enriched with gold thread and the car-* *touches have a variety of stitches. It has a bobbin-made vandyke edging of lace* (merletti a fuselli) *with gold thread introduced into it (167 cm long × 56 cm wide – 5 ft 6 in. × 22 in.). The work is Italian of the sixteenth century*

in a coffer unmounted, and 538 worked with rosettes and blossoms. There are references also to the skill of Mary Queen of Scots and her ladies in making such squares as well as many other pieces of embroidery, during her imprisonment. Many of these were presented to those she hoped might further her cause.

Because of the doubt about the dating we may – or may not – have reached back to lace work of the fifteenth century, but certainly have come to the time for which so little evidence is available that opinions differ sharply as to whether anything made then might be called

lace. Some of the earliest pieces on view in the Victoria and Albert Museum are seen in figures 54a and b and are given as German of the fourteenth and fifteenth centuries. The band of heraldic embroidery with its many shields made by darning on silk net with coloured silks may be of interest to heraldic artists but makes no pretence of being lace. The piece below, because of its fine silk net on which are stars and triangles, differently coloured, might be described as having a 'lacy' appearance but no higher claim could be made for it. Yet it is only a fragment, showing that some kind of darning on net must have been

made, so there might have been other work of a possibly higher standard.

The geometric designs give a very different effect. In the photograph the background cannot be distinguished: the darning would be with silver and gilt threads. It is the designs which seem to me important. The shapes within the octagonals are very like some copied and used by me, many years ago, when they were on display in the Museum and three can be seen in figures 34–35. They were then described as German of the sixteenth century. This piece is evidence of a well-established tradition of similar designs worked in the linen darning stitch, a century earlier. Its metal threads have ensured its survival when linen and even silk would have perished: however, one would think of it more as embroidery, not lace, although these pieces have been referred to as lacis, in the past.

Mrs Palliser has a reference to netted work, in an Italian document of 1493, where the inventory of articles from the wardrobes of two sisters included 'veils of good network' as well as articles in 'a reticella and a groppé'. So this is considered as the earliest written record of Italian lace.

A century earlier in England an Act of 1363 forbade that veils should be worn of silk or any other material except that made in the kingdom. They appear to have been 'a sort of network similar to the caul of Queen Philippa as seen on her tomb in Westminster Abbey'. The query as to what other threads might have been used reminds one of the netted caps of thread worked in with gold and silver by the Wadstone nuns in the early fourteenth century where the convent of St Bridget)

53(a–d) Patterns from Federico Vinciolo's book Renaissance Patterns for Lace and Embroidery, *1587*

was said to be celebrated for its lace.
Another item of network mentioned by
Mrs Palliser is the 'silver net work col-
lar' in the inventory of the Duke of
Burgundy in 1393.

In her book *Lacis*[9] 'Carita' mentions
'the cushion of network that St Paul's
Cathedral possessed in 1295 and three
pieces of the same work that were in
use in Exeter Cathedral in 1327.' On
the Continent during this period of the
thirteenth and fourteenth centuries the
names given to network were *opus filatorium* and *opus araneum*, the latter in
English meaning spiderwork; connecting it with the story of Ariadne (or
Arachne).

Thus far I have avoided using the
term 'lace' of these early periods. It is
realised that often when used in in-
ventories, letters etc, it refers to ornamented braids and cords. Mrs Palliser[10]
referred to a manuscript of 1651 which
'gives specimens of the laces such as
they were, stitched side by side with the
directions, which at once establishes the
fact that the laces of silk and gold, laces
of thread, were nothing more than
braids or cords – the laces used with
tags, commonly called "poynts" (the
ferrets of Anne of Austria) for fastening
the dresses, as well as for ornament,
previous to the introduction of pins. . . .
These double laces of ribbons and silk
were but plaited, a simple ornament still
used by the peasant women in some
countries of Europe.' From this followed the suggestion by Mrs Palliser
that these 'lace tags' in the course of
time could have been improved upon by
an edging and other stitchery, and so
have developed into a 'rude lace,
clumsy at first, and after a season improved upon.'

Whether or not this could have been
the origin of other lace forms, it could
hardly have become lacis, which needs a
netted foundation.

In fact, in their Historical Summary the authors, the Misses Mincoff and Marriage[11] do not support this idea. They describe braids such as the above as silken strings, from 3 mm to 13 mm ($\frac{1}{8}$ in. to $\frac{1}{2}$ in.) broad and say that though plaited threads or cords had been used for trimming all through the Middle Ages there are no traces of lace before the end of the fifteenth century, and that these first traces are more than doubtful. Actual specimens of lace of course bear no evidence of date. (The reference is to pillow ie bobbin laces.)

While still discussing pillow lace they make the complaint about the dozens of technical names rife in the fifteenth and sixteenth centuries for every kind of needlework. Continual confusions had arisen because the historical side had mostly been dealt with by men, or by women unversed in the technique: while 'those who have practical knowledge have seldom the learning or the inclination to make researches in archives or museums.'

Mrs Palliser too is concerned about the confusion in the use of terms. 'The term *laces* rendered in the English translation of the statutes (. . . of Edward IV) as "laces" implying braids . . . appears long before lace, properly so called, came into use. The earlier laces, such as they were, were defined by the term "passement" – a general term for gimps and braids as well as for lace. Modern industry has separated these two classes of work, but their being formerly so confounded renders it difficult in historical research to separate one from another.' In France also there was the same confusion, where 'passement' was applied to all varieties of lace, and where the 'passementiers' in control of the lace trade 'applied the same terms to their different products, whatever the material.'

A possible historical clue which it

54(a) Part of a band of heraldic embroidery silk net darned with coloured silks, German of fourteenth century (Victoria and Albert Museum, ref. 326, London)
(b) Fragment of fourteenth- or fifteenth-century silk net darned with coloured silks (Brock Collection, Victoria and Albert Museum, ref. 8254, London)

seemed to me ought to be investigated was a quotation from the *Ancien Riwle (Ancien Wisse)* given in *Seven Centuries of Lace*. The version in the text of the Corpus MS (edited by J R R Tolkien for the Early English Text Society, 1962, page 215) may be modernised as 'Make no purses . . . nor coifs nor silken bandages, nor *laz* without leave; but shape and sew and mend church vestments and poor men's garments'.

Examining the context in the version of the Corpus MS, I found instructions that the Apostle said that women should cover their heads but said nothing about wimples; that they should have no 'ring nor brooch . . . nor gloves'.

So my impression was that the *laz* would refer to another activity involving too much concentration on something that was ornamental instead of useful sewing and mending. It seemed to me likely that if braids were meant *laz* should also be in the plural, with

purses, and as we saw it – *laces* – in the statutes.

Through the kindness of the Secretary, in Oxford, of the Early English Text Society my questionings reached Professor Dobson, now the accepted expert on *Ancien Riwle (Ancien Wisse)*. With a most generous giving of his time and special knowledge very detailed replies were sent to me, examining different texts and translations, and this special passage.

'It is impossible to say for certain whether *laz* is meant as plural or singular, though I still think that *laz* is in fact a plural.'

Professor Dobson later elaborated what this might mean for my purpose of trying to trace definite references to lacework. 'Though his *laz* may mean (as I think) "braids", there may well have been lace work (the type of fabric) which he may have known about but which he may have called by some

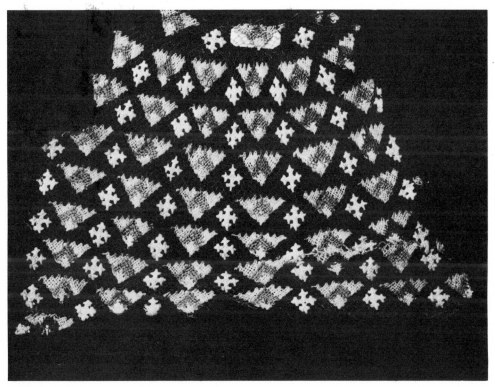

other word. Or he may have associated lace-work with braids so closely that he thought by forbidding "braids" he was also forbidding lace-work. . . . By saying that I think that *laz* means "braids" and is a plural, I certainly do not mean that lace-work did not exist—merely that you cannot directly cite this word as evidence for the existence of lace-work. But there must have been some reason why he forbade the making of "braids" and the reason must be that it involved some elaborate sort of needlework (since that is what the whole passage is about).'

By drawing attention to a sentence later in the same context Professor Dobson gave another interesting clue. 'None of you shall *criblin* for love or money', where *criblin* is taken to mean 'do sieve-work', (from its relation to the French 'cribler' to sieve.) The query is what 'sieve-work' may mean in needlework terms—obviously something very elaborate and therefore very unsuitable. A suggestion had been made by J. Hall that it must mean some kind of openwork—filatorium (on net), drawn thread, or tambour, with the idea that such work might be used for ornamenting altar cloths or pyx cloths or even albs.

However, with our knowledge of the sixteenth century Buratto work (figures 36, 37, 38) which was darned on a loosely woven linen gauge ground like that used for sieving, one is aware that this sounds the most likely explanation of the occupation known as '*criblin*'. And narrow bands or edgings of it would be very suitable for use on articles used at the altar.

Dare one suggest that here there is reference to a form of lace being made in England, in 1235?

Additional information given in Professor Dobson's letters is most valuable in helping us to understand the situation. For the women who were being exhorted to a simple life were not nuns living in a convent but a small group of anchoresses. These would be people who had withdrawn from the world for religious reasons, and from whose guidance this *Ancien Riwle (Ancien Wisse)* had been prepared.

In wondering what happened to lace-making during the years before the fifteenth century we need to remember that the fourteenth century was the time of the disastrous plague of the Black Death, especially when we regret the change in England, from the earlier century (about 1250–1350) of its fame for *opus Anglicanum*, responsible for such embroideries as the Syon Cope.

So many of these and other vestments have survived the centuries partly because they were of such value as to be kept for special ceremonial occasions and partly because their silk, with gold and silver threads, would not be laundered. The nuns and monks responsible for such fine work would also be concerned with providing all the linen cloths for use at the altars. Though these could be expected to have a comparatively short life yet their symbolic importance would mean that they also would be beautified by fine stitchery. On linen this might be by work on counted threads, by pulled work, by drawn-thread work. From the latter may have developed the reticella lace designs and the *punto in aria*, even, it has been suggested, the lacis. Remembering, again, that a knotted net ground is needed for this, I cannot agree.

The net ground brings us to a consideration of the references to net-work in Greek, Egyptian (especially Coptic) and other Eastern texts, with Biblical examples. One theory suggests that these describe a decoration made by the twisting of threads, a technique now known by the Swedish name of 'sprang'. For pieces of hair-nets, caps and stockings were found in peat-bogs in Denmark and Norway and dated as of the Bronze Age, ie between 1500 and 1100 BC. So articles found in Egyptian graves of the Coptic period (fourth–fifth century AD) are also said to be made by that process, not by netting.

The frontispiece of Margaret Maidment's book[12] shows a piece of this plaited work from Upper Egypt, and her first chapter gives a detailed account of how this would be made, and takes it as 'a step towards bobbin lace'. She states clearly that the fragments found at Heraklopolis Magna and other tombs show two distinct kinds of work. 'One kind is of netting in which each crossing of threads is fastened by a knot. Evidently 'filet' lace originated from this. The other kind . . . consists of twisted threads without knots and seems more likely to be the origin of bobbin made lace.'

With such possibilities in mind one recalls that two books, in considering the history of lace making in Europe, give the opinion that its origin may be traced back to Eastern sources. The Misses Mincoff and Marriage[13] point out that 'the first published patterns show a fully developed technique': that a native growth would have shown 'more tentative, clumsy beginnings both in the pattern books and in the specimens of old Venice lace still surviving, not the graceful, complex designs that lie before us.' They refer also to the Oriental character in the arabesques that form the designs, and to the fact that Venice was the chief European port for trade with the East. They conclude, 'But if for the present there is no decisive proof of the Eastern origin of pillow lace, at least the evidence is strong in its favour.'

It appears to me that there is an even stronger case for connecting the origin and development of lacis with Eastern sources.

From a detailed study of the designs in the early printed books, and especially from her personal examination of the 'Assisi Alb and the Boniface Alb' Mrs Hungerford Pollen[14] found, in the latter, 'lace ornaments of an Eastern character' with repeated geometrical patterns symmetrically grouped in squares and worked by the needle in *punto a rammendo* (ie darning stitch as used in lacis work). On the Assisi Alb she found that the lace-work is worked on the linen itself in *tela tirata* (drawn thread) a *punto reale* (ie satin stitch). The introduction of symbolic animals and chimeras, and particularly the polygonal character of the designs established, she considered, its Coptic derivation.

In the study of the symbolism of designs, Chapter 5, we shall see that the use in early Christian art, including embroidery and lace, of the emblems of the cross and the gammadion (swastika) derived ultimately from Eastern sources many centuries earlier.

It is not only from the study of the designs that one is led to consider the importance of Eastern sources for decorated net work. Our earlier references to veils of network were from the fourteenth and fifteenth centuries AD. But Homer wrote about 'her veil of airy texture, work of her own hand' (*Iliad* VIII). In the Biblical accounts of the furnishings for the Tabernacle (Exodus XXVI v 31) the 'vail' is described which was to separate 'the most holy place'.

In a tomb of Egypto-Roman period at Fayoun in Middle Egypt was found a round net apparently made of a dark brown silk by the use of different sized meshes. Patterns were made by increasings and decreasings, repeated alternately, as the nineteenth century ladies made their d'oyleys.

In Egyptian mythology the net had

symbolic meanings. The Goddess Net, or Neith was, in one form the goddess of the loom and the shuttle and also of the chase. Thus came the later connection with the Greek Goddess Athene, the patron of spinning and weaving, and hence her anger at the 'web' made by Arachne, depicting stories of the Gods; and this ended in Arachne's death and her being changed into a spider. So another name for the net-work – *opus filatorium* – of the ninth to thirteenth centuries was *opus araneum*, ie spider work.

But do we need a mythical tale to see a resemblance between a spider's web and a piece of fine netting, which can have a gossamer-like appearance? Some needlewomen are now recovering the delight of producing circles of netting, 'weaving' their own variations of design as the work progresses. I could wish for netting to be accepted as a definite form of lace work. It is surprising how simple variations can result in delightful fine lace edgings. An old *Weldon*'s book on netting illustrated many such.

For purely decorative purposes there could be pendant mobiles in fine threads, or heavier hangings and curtains. You may not want to enclose the whole bed with hangings and valances of undarned net, known as reseau (or rexil etc), as listed in inventory and wardrobe accounts of the sixteenth century. But might it not provide a pleasant innovation for a dividing curtain for an 'open-plan' living room, especially if colours were used to match the décor?

Of the many methods of developing patterns in net a few are offered in the instruction chapter. For those whose preferences are for abstract rather than patterned regularity in decoration the possibilities are endless of introducing a variety of textures and threads. For

such work, included under the term 'needle lace' Mrs Virginia Churchill Bath[15] in her book *Lace* offers inspiration. Not for me this 'unchartered freedom'. My preference has been for work needing a precision and formal preparation of designs, with the kind of discipline required in its accurate development.

To return to our netting: as a traditional activity its origins would probably be prehistoric, when nets were made for the practical purpose of trapping fish and animals for food. Plant fibres were surely in early use, for primitive people still twist, plait and coil them in complicated ways into useful bowls or just for personal ornaments, of bracelets and pendants. I have such articles, as well as mats, bought many years ago from Zulus in South Africa and they are still firm and useful.

Such traditional skills are part of the human inheritance. Children's fingers will eagerly make loops and chains and knots. How many kinds does a Boy Scout learn, and how many articles are thus produced from simple materials? It is as if there were some physical remembrance of the necessary movements and so a pleasure in relearning (or recalling?) them. Netting is one of the activities which can provide that sensation. I have been aware of it also in the handling of bobbins for lace making.

Thus in reviving a primitive facility we may even be re-interpreting for ourselves and for others activities which can give a deep satisfaction to some universal urge to organise and fashion the substances provided by Nature into ordered and artistic creation.

Perhaps such ideas may inspire people to pass on to the practical instructions in the following chapter, and learn to make the netting knot.

Netting Instructions

Threads

The purpose for which the piece of netting is to be used will determine the kind of thread needed. If it is to be for filet lace (lacis) then by far the best for appearance and permanent value are linen threads, now again obtainable.

Old lacis was often made on net of a finer thread than that used for the design: some people prefer to use the same thickness for both. At one time only coarse linen threads were available, and then the knots, whose presence form part of the effect, were too evident, making a background of a rough texture.

For articles to be made by netting cotton there are many advantages, especially in the variety of colours and the range of thickness available (from 1 to 150 now). But the very fine threads may break when pulled firmly to make the knot: also cottons are apt to twist into tight little knots in the working thread. A different result will be obtained by the use of soft mercerised cotton threads. Many of these are now supplied eg DMC Cordonnet, Brillante D'Alsace, Retour D'Alsace, Coton Perlé. Fancy threads such as Goldfingering, Moonlight and Soirée make attractive collars (figures 63, 64) etc. Knitting cottons such as Lyscord, Lyscordet, Suzette, Wendy can be used for netting various mats, then to be darned (figures 76, 77) and for curtains.

String and macramé would be suitable for such articles as shopping bags and table tennis nets: while for use in the garden specially treated twines would be needed to prevent rotting. However for some of these latter purposes probably the simpler 'fisherman's knot' would be more suitable.

Meshes or gauges

These regulate the size of the loops of the netting and so must be made of a firm substance, not to bend or break, and must be an even breadth along the length. Those now sold as 'antiques' were made of bone or ivory, the finest circular, but mostly flat. Attractive ivory carved cases to hold meshes and needles may still be found, figure 55. For fine filet net knitting needles are useful, of sizes 12, 13, and 14. A modern man-made material is used to make meshes from 3 mm ($\frac{1}{8}$ in.) in breadth.

Needles

Netting needles have been made of steel, ivory, or wood of lengths of 13 cm–25 cm (5 in.–10 in.) and varying in thickness. Both ends are hollowed out, yet meeting closely together at the points so that the thread wound round the length does not slip out. (This will happen if too much thread has been frequently used on the needle, so forcing the 'prongs' open.) These may now

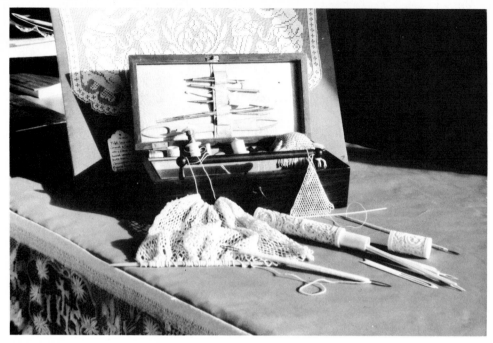

55 *Mahogany box with weighted bottom and special rod for holding the netting whilst working (Mrs Purvis's Collection)*

be bought, individually handmade, to order, in steel or ivory, though for years they have not been obtainable (figure 56). A long bodkin can be used, or a 'double long darner' if one first blunts its point. That only allows for short lengths of thread, and so will mean more knots.

Support

The conventional way of anchoring the work has been to use either a 'stirrup' of ribbon or string held round the foot, or to have a box or cushion heavily weighted (with lead), the former being a place to store the tools.

Old attractively carved clamps suggested to me the use of a small metal clamp. This can be attached to any firm table and is easily removed and stored. Partly to prevent marking a table and also to hold a few useful large-headed pins, I place a small piece of felt under

the clamp and a similar sized piece of card beneath the table. Any firm basis can be used which will resist the pull needed by the worker to tighten the knots.

Netting

Many people have found written instructions on how to make netting difficult to follow, for they do sound complicated.

Essentially one is making three loops with the thread and they form a figure 8 over the mesh and fingers, being held in that position (a) by the thumb, (b) by the first three fingers, (c) by the little finger. The knot is formed when one releases the loops in turn, beginning with that under the thumb, then from the grouped fingers and lastly from the little finger.

So, to begin: a small loop of strong string is tied to the clamp, and another loop (say about 15 cm–20 cm (6 in.– 8 in.) long) is tied to that by a simple knot to be undone when the work is finished. For that reason this last thread may be slightly thicker than that to be used for the net.

Tie the working thread to the loop, again with a single knot and leaving a piece about 20 cm (8 in.) long. This will be needed, when a square piece is made, to join together the first two loops. It is useful to tie this loosely higher up the loop to prevent it being in the way of the working.

A small piece of netting has been prepared for the demonstration of making the knot: for that is more clearly seen than if shown from the commencement.

Hold the mesh horizontally in the left hand between the thumb and first fingers, close up to the netting. In the right hand have the needle ready, having left about 46 cm (18 in.) of thread unwound.

Bring the thread down over the *front* of the mesh, round the first three fingers, and over to the left, to be held there firmly by the thumb (figure 57a). Next make a loop going up, and then coming down *behind the mesh*, ready for figure 57b.

Here the needle is taken up through the loop held by the fingers, *behind* the mesh and into the next loop (of the prepared net). The little finger, (which I usually keep tucked out of the way) now grasps the thread and holds it firmly while the needle is pulled through, the thumb releases its loop, and the thread is drawn close to the mesh (figure 57c).

Next the three fingers let go of their loop, while the working thread is pulled again close to the mesh. Now only the loop held by the little finger remains (figure 57d). Very gradually (until expert) ease this loop off the little finger while holding the mesh firmly against the row of worked net. Pull the thread tight to make the knot. It is the control of this last movement which produces

the even loops in the netting.

Because it has usually been pictured with three fingers holding the first loop I have repeated that process here. But I normally use only the two first fingers there, as easier to be released. Doubtless netters will find some variations to suit themselves for quicker working. Practice is needed (as with all skills); once mastered it can be a relaxing activity, with its own rhythm, and needing just enough concentration to prevent one's mind from thinking about other problems in life. Children often learn it more quickly than adults.

This netting knot is so secure that the loops formed by it remain complete even when the thread is cut close to the knot. Any part of the net may be cut across and edges may be shaped into 'vandyke' points for a lace edging (figure 58). Naturally this also means that the knot is difficult to unpick, so there is a use for pins ready by the clamp. When being worked, if there seems any doubt as to some mistake being made it is wise to take back the needle through the loops and begin the knot again.

The illustration (figure 59) shows a piece of netting begun with two stitches, then with increases, eventually to form a square or oblong piece. It will be seen that two rows of netting give a diamond shape where the edge has been stretched to show the squares that will be formed when the piece is completed.

For the first attempt at netting it might be helpful to make about ten loops into the formation chain and work to and fro on these without any increasing. One nets always from left to right, so at the end of each row, when the mesh is withdrawn, the work is turned over to the left. For the first stitch of

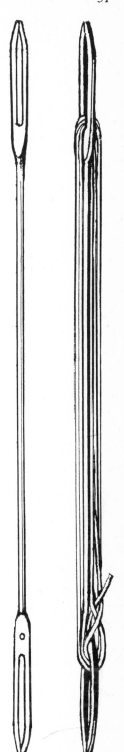

56 *Steel netting needles, one wound with thread*

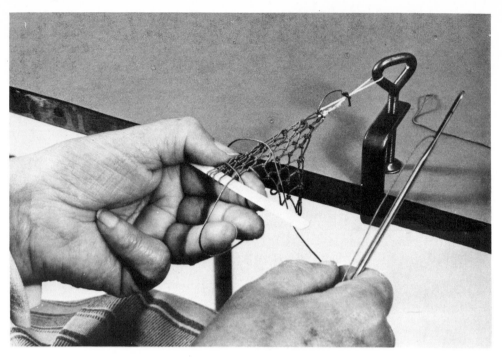

*57 (a) and (b) Netting showing the first
position of the hands and mesh with first
movement*

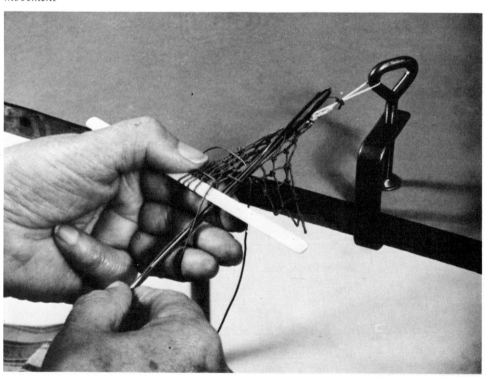

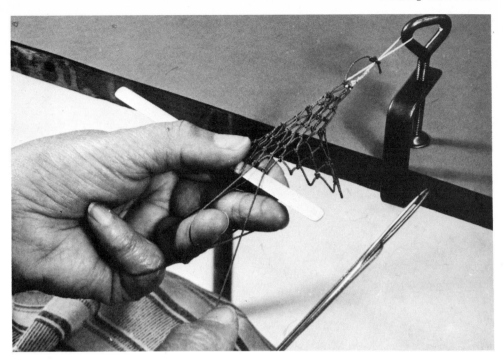

(c) Second movement
*(d) Position ready for final release of
thread from the little finger to close the
knot*

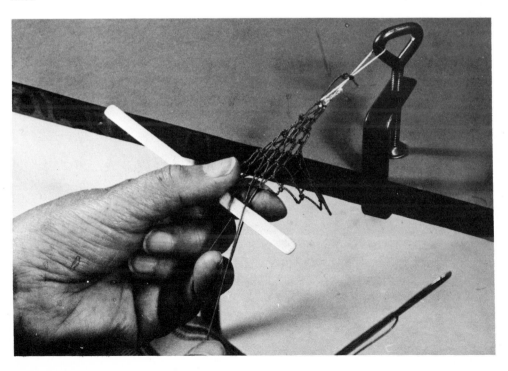

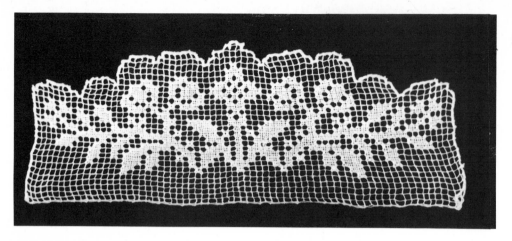

58 *Lace with vandyke edging buttonholed and the net cut*

59 *Netting showing beginning and also square and oblong pieces*

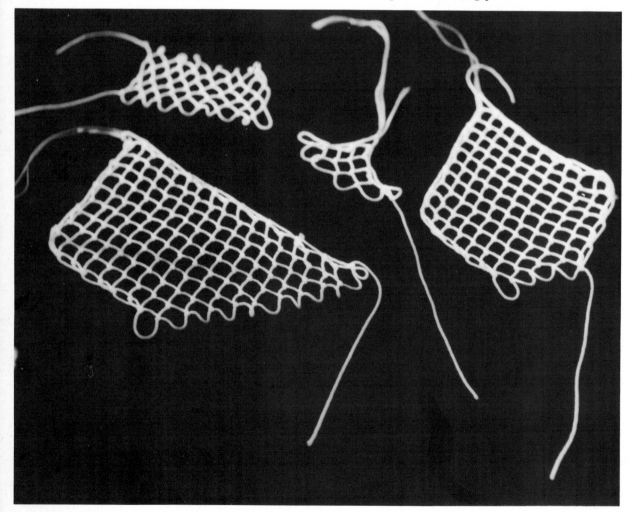

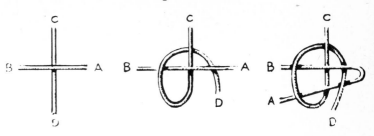

60 *Weaver's knot*

the next row the mesh must be held firmly close to the edge of the hanging loop while the thread is passed round the fingers and the needle inserted into what was the last loop of the previous row, for the next knot to be made. Joins in the working thread should be made by either the well-known weaver's knot (figure 60) or the lace knot (figure 61). The latter shows a loop made by the fingers with the new thread (A–B) and the position for the old thread (C–D) inside it. A sharp pull separates the thread A–B to grip it round C–D, and a slight click can be heard. Make quite sure by pulling all ends tightly before cutting them off close to the knot now formed. Whenever possible arrange for such joins in the thread to occur at the end of a row of netting.

An unusual specimen of Dutch filet lace is illustrated in figure 18, page 19. Here the net is used with the *diamond* shapes which are darned to produce the flower and curving leaf design. But more well-known is the lace on squared net.

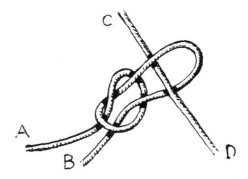

61 *Lace knot*

To make a square piece of netting
Begin with two stitches on the foundation thread. *Increase* by making two stitches into the last loop of each row until there are loops numbering one more than the intended number for each side of the finished square.

Do *one row* without any increase.

Second half – Decrease by taking two loops together at the end of every row until only two remain.

Join these two by making the usual preparations for the knot, but by withdrawing the mesh before the thread is pulled tight. The first two stitches of the beginning will need to be joined.

To make an oblong piece of netting
Begin as for a square piece, with two stitches, *increasing* at the end of each row until there are *two more* loops made than the number of holes required for the width of the oblong.

Increase at the end of the next row, and *decrease* at the end of the next one – that is alternately increasing and decreasing. When the longer side is the desired length take *two loops together* at the end of *every row* until two loops remain. Join these two and the original two at the beginning (see figure 59).

When making either a square or an oblong the increases produce smaller loops shortening that edge. So a very slight looseness is needed there.

The pulling on the work when netting will result in a diamond-shaped piece. After having been soaked in water it can be stretched into a better shape, first with the fingers and then with a light moderately warm iron.

Attaching it to a frame, with an over-sewing preferably into each square, stretching the net while doing so, will usually be all that is needed to produce a good shape. I have found this is easiest if two adjacent sides are first firmly joined to the frame; then the net can be pulled taut from them while the other two sides are attached. The wire frame needs to be bound first with strong ribbon or bias binding. For small pieces of lace wooden picture frames can be used, but larger ones in wood may not be rigid enough unless the corners are

62 Small wooden picture frame used to work a piece of lacis

strengthened (figure 62).

For those of us who were making filet lace fifty years ago there could be bought in London linen hand-knotted net, made by peasants on the Continent. It varied in quality: but what amazed me was the usual regularity even in yards of the net.

When learning to make the net myself I found, as so many others do, that it needed a considerable amount of practice. Instead of producing many scraps not good enough to use for lace work it is more pleasurable to obtain facility in working the knots by making attractive and useful articles such as collars, mats and narrow edgings on handkerchiefs. Here the absolute evenness of the loops is neither noticeable nor so important, while one becomes familiar with the results of using different threads and different sized meshes. Such work was popular in the early 1900s for d'oyleys either completely netted or made round a circle of linen. Now, with such a variety of threads being produced, such as those partly metallic, there are many delightful ways of becoming a proficient netter.

The two collars illustrated in figures 63 and 64 were worked in *Goldfingering*, which can be bought in several colours. Because net always stretches, a crochet heading is used first; then this is attached to a firm cushion (or lace pillow if already possessed) in a curve in about six places by long glass-headed pins. These will be removed when each row is finished to allow the net to be turned over, remembering that netting is worked from left to right.

Details

Meshes 5 mm ($\frac{3}{16}$ in.), 6 mm ($\frac{1}{4}$ in.), 9 mm ($\frac{3}{8}$ in.). Steel netting needle (or long bodkin).
Crochet hook – steel 00. Silver *Goldfingering*.

Crochet a chain of 93, turning to miss 1 chain, for 92 stitches.
Crochet 1 row in dc and 1 row in treble. (The latter gives spaces into which the netting needle will easily pass.) (figure 63).

Netting

	Mesh 5 mm ($\frac{3}{16}$ in.)	Net 3 rows plain
Row 4	Mesh 5 mm ($\frac{3}{16}$ in.)	Net 2 stitches into each loop
Row 5	Mesh 6 mm ($\frac{1}{4}$ in.)	Net 2 together all along
Row 6	Mesh 6 mm ($\frac{1}{4}$ in.)	Net 2 stitches into each loop
Row 7	Mesh 6 mm ($\frac{1}{4}$ in.)	(Net 1 plain, net 3 together) and repeat the bracket all along
Row 8	Mesh 9 mm ($\frac{3}{8}$ in.)	*Twisted Netting* ie net 1 in the 2nd loop, 1 in the first loop, net 1 in the 4th loop, net 1 in the 3rd, etc
Row 9	Mesh 6 mm ($\frac{1}{4}$ in.)	(Net 1 in the small loop, net 3 in the large loop) and repeat the bracket
Row 10	Mesh 5 mm ($\frac{3}{16}$ in.)	Net 2 together all along
Row 11	Mesh 5 mm ($\frac{3}{16}$ in.)	Net 2 together all along

Length 43 cm (17 in.) Depth 8 cm (3 in.) approximately

A longer or shorter collar can be made by varying the length of chain made

Another collar, figure 64, made in bronze *Goldfingering* has a looser, lacier effect.

Details

Meshes 3 mm ($\frac{1}{8}$ in.), 9 mm ($\frac{3}{8}$ in.), 6 mm ($\frac{1}{4}$ in.), 15 mm ($\frac{5}{8}$ in.)
Steel crochet hook 00. Steel netting needle (or long bodkin) (figure 64).

Work a chain of 97 stitches, turning to miss 1 chain for 96 stitches
Work 1 row dc and 1 row treble

Netting

	Mesh 5 mm ($\frac{3}{16}$ in.)	4 rows plain netting
Row 5	Mesh 6 mm ($\frac{1}{4}$ in.)	(Net 3 in first loop, 3 in next, net 2 plain) repeat the bracket to the end
Row 6	Mesh 6 mm ($\frac{1}{4}$ in.)	(Net 3 plain, take 5 together) and repeat to the end
Row 7	Mesh 5 mm ($\frac{3}{16}$ in.)	Plain netting
Row 8	Mesh 5 mm ($\frac{3}{16}$ in.)	Plain netting
Row 9	Mesh 6 mm ($\frac{1}{4}$ in.)	(Net 2 plain, 3 in next loop, 3 in next) and repeat to end
Row 10	Mesh 6 mm ($\frac{1}{4}$ in.)	(Net 5 together, net 3 plain) and repeat to end
Row 11	Mesh 5 mm ($\frac{3}{16}$ in.)	Plain netting
Row 12	Mesh 15 mm ($\frac{5}{8}$ in.)	Net 2 into each loop
Row 13	Mesh 3 mm ($\frac{1}{8}$ in.)	Plain netting
Row 14	Mesh 3 mm ($\frac{1}{8}$ in.)	(Net 5 plain, miss 1 loop) repeat to end
Row 15	Mesh 3 mm ($\frac{1}{8}$ in.)	(Net 4 plain, miss 1 loop) repeat to end
Row 16	Mesh 3 mm ($\frac{1}{8}$ in.)	(Net 3 plain, miss 1 loop) repeat to end
Row 17	Mesh 3 mm ($\frac{1}{8}$ in.)	(Net 2 plain, miss 1 loop) repeat to end

Length 48 cm (19$\frac{1}{2}$ in.) Depth 10 cm (4 in.) approximately

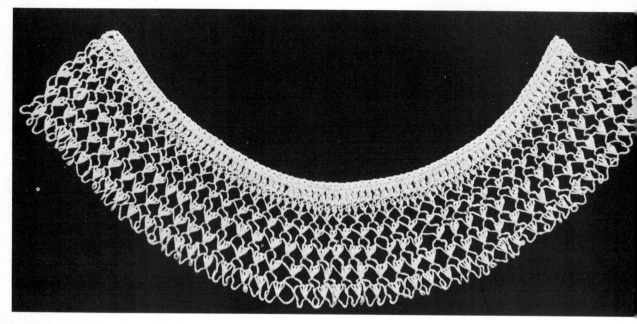

63 Netted collar worked in silver
Goldfingering

64 Netted collar worked in bronze
Goldfingering

It is a simple matter to vary the sizes of the meshes used, and by alternating plain rows with patterns formed by netting several times into a loop, and on the next row joining some together, to make up one's own designs for the size and shape desired. Other examples are given with a jabot also (figures 65 and 66).

In old pattern books published by Weldons there are many illustrations of patterns of netting, named 'looped netting, sprig netting, spike netting, leaf netting', and others, all developments of the same process. If broad meshes are used they could make attractive short curtains.

In fact there are historical references to the use of plain netting, called Reseau (or Rezel, Rezuel) as early as the fourteenth century, for curtains and bed hangings.

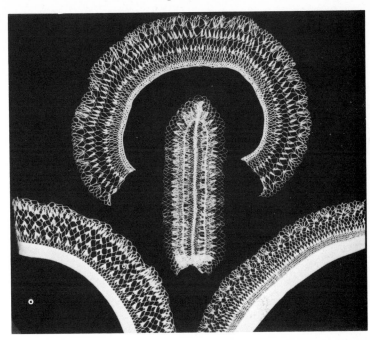

65 Jabot and collars worked in fine linen threads

66 One section of a netted collar in two parts worked in fine linen thread

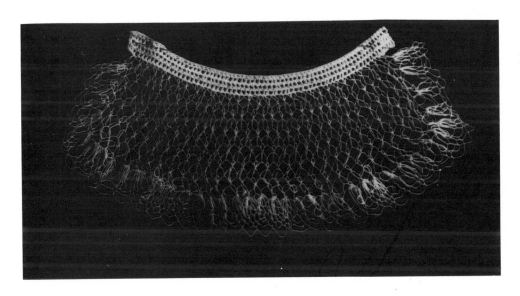

Garden hat – netted

Thread DMC Coton Perlé no. 5 or Campbell's Linen no. 40
Ribbon 90 cm (1 yd)
Netting needle
15 cm or 18 cm (6 in. or 7 in.) long

Meshes
15 mm and 6 mm ($\frac{5}{8}$ in. and $\frac{1}{4}$ in.)
   Begin with about a 46 cm (18 in.) length of thread (the 'tail').

	Mesh	
Row 1	15 mm ($\frac{5}{8}$ in.)	Work 19 loops. Close and form the 20th loop by tying together the 'tail' and the shuttle thread at the bottom of the loop. Close each row in the same manner by tying the 'tail' with the shuttle thread to form the last loop of each row.

	Mesh			Mesh	
Rows 2 and 3	15 mm ($\frac{5}{8}$ in.)	Net 1 in each loop.	Row 4	15 mm ($\frac{5}{8}$ in.)	Net 2 in each loop.
Row 5	15 mm ($\frac{5}{8}$ in.)	Net 1 in each loop.	Row 6	15 mm ($\frac{5}{8}$ in.)	Net 2 in each loop.
Row 7	15 mm ($\frac{5}{8}$ in,)	Net 1 in each loop.	Row 8	15 mm ($\frac{5}{8}$ in.)	Net 3 together all round.
Row 9	15 mm ($\frac{5}{8}$ in.)	Net 3 in each loop.	Row 10	15 mm ($\frac{5}{8}$ in.)	(Net 1 in 1 loop, net 2 together) repeat to end.
Rows 11, 12, 13	6 mm ($\frac{1}{4}$ in.)	Net 1 in each loop.	Row 14	15 mm ($\frac{5}{8}$ in.)	Net 1 in each loop.
Row 15	15 mm ($\frac{5}{8}$ in.)	Net 2 together.	Row 16	15 mm ($\frac{5}{8}$ in)	Net 3 in each loop.
Rows 17, 18, 19	6 mm ($\frac{1}{4}$ in.)	Net 1 in each loop.	Row 20	15 mm ($\frac{5}{8}$ in.)	Net 1 in each loop.
Row 21	15 mm ($\frac{5}{8}$ in.)	Net 2 together.	Row 22	15 mm ($\frac{5}{8}$ in.)	Net 5 in each loop.
Rows 23, 24, 25, 26	6 mm ($\frac{1}{4}$ in.)	Net 1 in each loop.	Row 27	15 mm ($\frac{5}{8}$ in.)	Net 1 in each loop.
Row 28	15 mm ($\frac{5}{8}$ in.)	Net 3 together.	Row 29	15 mm ($\frac{5}{8}$ in.)	Net 6 in each loop.
Row 30	15 mm ($\frac{5}{8}$ in.)	(Net 1, net 1, net 2 together) repeat to end.			
Row 31	15 mm ($\frac{5}{8}$ in.)	(Net 3 in 1 loop, 1 in next, 1 in next) repeat to end.			
Row 32	6 mm ($\frac{1}{4}$ in.)	Net 1 in each loop.			

Stiffen, tie off and block. Add ribbon band.

To shape a block
Make a hard cylinder of material and cover it with foil, shaped 13 cm (5$\frac{1}{4}$ in.) at the top, and 18 cm (7 in.) at the bottom, and 11 cm (4$\frac{1}{2}$ in.) high. Stiffen.
   Dry near the prepared mould.

Pin the hat round the 18 cm (7 in.) base. Flatten the brim and pin it all round.
   The ribbon is threaded through rows 14, 15 and 16, after the hat is dried. It can be adjusted a little to the required size of the head by stretching, if needed, at the time of blocking.

67 *Netted garden hat (made by Mrs Cragun)*

This hat was made and the instructions given to me by Mrs Bertha Cragun of the USA. The 'star design' mat (figure 68) shows an original design by Mrs Cragun who has unusual ideas for using the netting, eg the attractive lady on the pillow slip, whose frilly gown is made from a circular d'oyley, with very full edge and cut into half to form the skirts (figure 69).

Lace edgings for handkerchiefs may be simple and narrow or deeper and more elaborate. The net is easily pulled into shape by the fingers after being laundered (figure 70).

A mat in multi-coloured crochet thread was made with a squared centre by regular increasings at four corners (figure 71).

Attractive lampshades can be made in netting, in sizes and colours of one's choice, varying the texture, close or loose, and shaping by increases and decreases in the netting (figure 72).

Figure 73 shows an interesting mixture of square and ornamental netting with pattern in needle darning stitch, possibly of Arabic origin.

68 *Netted mat in a star design (made by Mrs Cragun)*

69 *Netted d'oyley used to decorate a pillow slip (made by Mrs Cragun)*

70 *Narrow netted handkerchief edging*

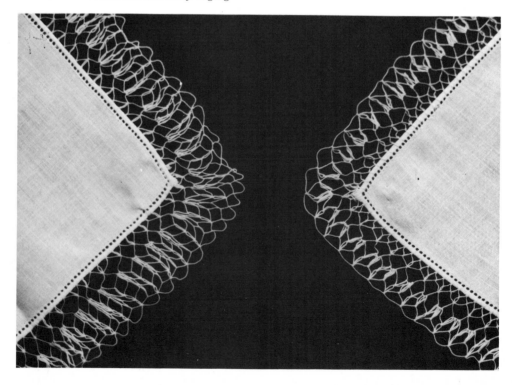

71 Netted mat worked in multi-coloured
no. 20 crochet thread

72 Netted lampshade worked in coloured
no. 20 crochet threads

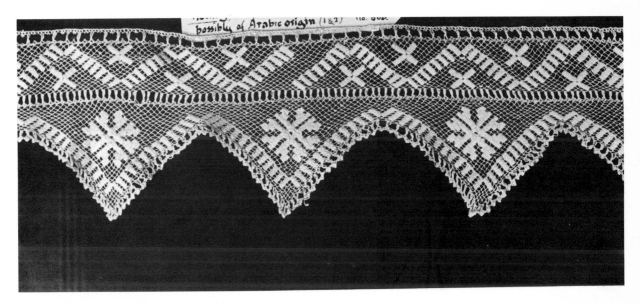

73 Lace design possibly of Arabic origin
(Mrs Purvis's Collection)

The Technique of Filet Lace

For filet ancien only two stitches were normally used: these are generally known as toile (or linen or cloth stitch) and reprise (or darning). The latter is the simpler, consisting only of passing the working thread over and under each thread of the net in a horizontal or vertical direction. This is shown very loosely worked on Sampler B and the effect produced is drawn in the diagram, figure 74. As the whole space is closely filled a much coarser thread is often used than that for the net, to avoid passing too frequently to and fro. The solid appearance yet gives an impression of light and shade: when used in combination with linen stitch there is a pleasing variety of texture. The different appearance of the stitches is shown on Sampler A where the same familiar design is worked by the two methods, while below a formal leaf shape uses both stitches.

What we would usually describe as darning is the linen stitch, where the first foundation threads passed over and under the line of the net, are then themselves crossed (figure 75). This will also be seen in the few spaces worked as for a possible corner use, on Sampler B and on the shapes below it and to the right.

One must always be careful to leave the foundation threads slightly loose when there is a solid extent of linen stitch; for the following movements of the thread will tighten them. Also it is unusual to meet, in old lace, linen stitch where the threads are run *twice* to and fro in the spaces; though this has sometimes been illustrated as if it were the normal linen or cloth stitch.

A later form of the lace, known as filet Richelieu in France and *punto filet* in Italy was popular during the Renaissance period (see figures 19–22). Here the linen stitch was outlined by a much thicker thread which often also formed a line of outline stitches joining parts of the design. This could give a lighter, lacier appearance. Attractive designs are used for mats (figures 76, 77) by combining toile and reprise with lace (loop) stitch.

The use of a variety of embroidery stitches on a filet net background was introduced during the nineteenth century as filet guipure (figures 78 and 79).

74 Reprise stitch

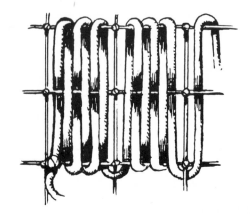

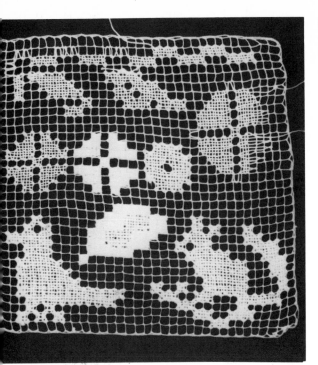

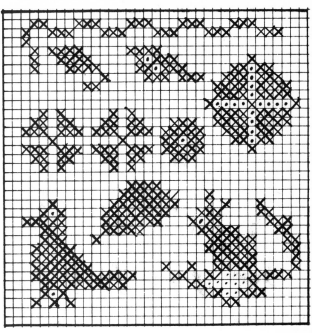

Sampler A

Sampler B

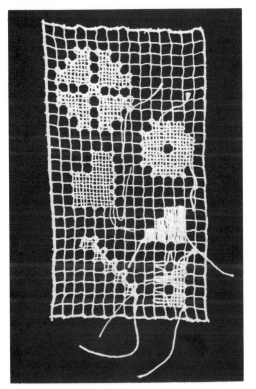

75 *A single toile (linen) stitch*

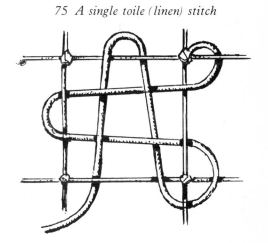

76 *Mat showing toile, reprise and loop stitches*

77 *Mat showing toile and embroidery stitches*

78 *Loop, star and Venetian stitches*
(Mrs Purvis's Collection)

79 *Filet guipure*

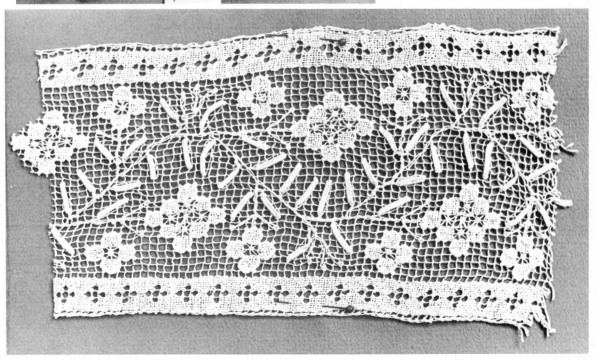

Edging

Every design of filet ancien has either a returning thread to edge the loops previously worked on the outside of the design, or else a second thread which was begun where the first commenced. For the correct following of the design will leave some parts not completed, and these must wait to be dealt with until this edging is worked. The border at the top of Sampler A is left unfinished to show this and it is seen on the five squares worked diagonally. Sometimes, when reaching a still-to-be-completed part, one sadly discovers that a mistake had been made there earlier in the work.

This edging, often omitted in examples and accounts given of filet, is most important, partly to pass from one part to another, and partly to strengthen the work and even the tension.

When planned by the artist-designers spaces were left empty within the patterns to suggest, for example, the veins of leaves, the shapes of flowers, and also to break the solidity of animal forms, as well as to indicate the flowing curves of costumes on human figures. These enclosed spaces were never to be crossed by the thread. Their beautifully rounded appearance was obtained by taking the thread round three directions of the compass before returning by the route by which it first entered the enclosed space. For my own clarification in working, and in explaining the method, I call such spaces 'holes' as distinct from areas which are not entirely closed in. In plotting the designs on graph paper (which should always be the preparation for working them) I always mark these holes with dots, preferably in a different coloured ink: for one needs to be kept constantly aware of their existence.

This correct method of dealing with holes produces an effect in a piece of lace which can be quickly discerned by an experienced eye, distinguishing those thus naturally rounded, planned in the designing, from the spaces often pulled taut by the thread on the line of the net, if not correctly worked.

Descriptions in words often confuse where diagrams will make one's meaning clearer. Figures 80a, b, c show the stages of completing a separate hole. In figure 80a the foundation thread is seen to pass through the first square, under and over the net, thus to enter the space to be enclosed (the hole). Here it moves one square to the west and back, then one north and back, then to the east and back (each time under and over the line of the net) and so coming back to the hole and down to where it entered the first square.

The next move is round the corner to the left. So in figure 80b the darning is seen, under and over the threads inside the squares, while those first threads are shown with a fainter, continuous line in order to distinguish them. The path now followed is marked by the heavy line, and this diagram also shows clearly the method of edging referred to earlier. For in the square to the middle right, as it passes over and under the net it also enters the loop of the first thread, and this is repeated when it reaches the following loops. Figure 80c gives the finish of the darning and edging as the end meets the beginning.

It would be unusual to have so small a shape, with a single hole, though often small circles are grouped, each with a central hole, when depicting a bunch of grapes – perhaps so suggesting the spot of light one sees on the fruit? Such a circle has been worked in the centre of Sampler A. Above it can be seen a leaf-like design whose two holes have been worked diagonally next to each other. Below, the bird and the squirrel each have a hole as the eyes. Both figures are

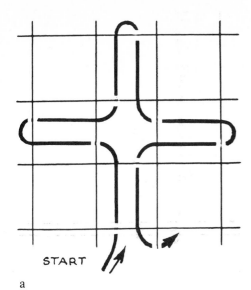

START

a

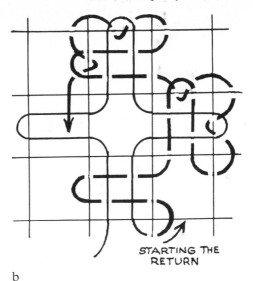

STARTING THE
RETURN

b

80(a) Diagram of a single 'hole'
*   Figures (b) and (c) show the working*
being completed

outlined by the edging threads as they
return to where they began, there to be
knotted with the end left at the beginning.

In the upper right hand side of
Sampler A is a design left uncompleted
where four triangular shapes enclose
rows of holes. It gives an important
and pleasant example of how to keep to
the design and learn, especially, how to
follow the direction of the thread. For
that purpose larger examples are shown
worked, in figures 81 and 82, the latter
the finished shape. In the unfinished
piece can be seen the beginning thread
loosely tied below the design, before it
began by entering the first two squares
at the left and so found itself in an
enclosed space and could not return.
The move was then out into the single
square at the left, back, up and back
two squares, up and back three, then
four, then four, to reach the single
space at the centre. Having worked
along this, the next two quarters of the
design were similarly threaded until

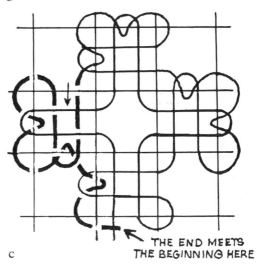

THE END MEETS
THE BEGINNING HERE

c

again reaching and passing through the
central square. Clearly the direction is
now down to fill the two sets of four
squares, next the three. Finally there
will be the second foundation thread
now laid in the two squares where the
work began. Here comes an important
point to note. For when the thread is
taken horizontally along the three
squares below, it again enters a row of
holes and must not return to darn, but
move into the *row above* and darn that,
where the needle is left in to stress its
positioning.

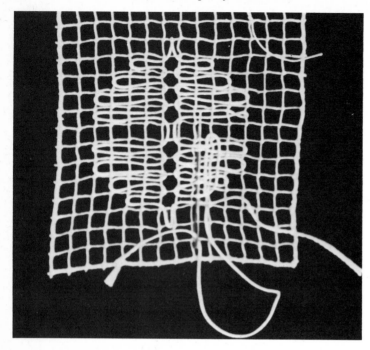

81 Partly worked design

82 Completion of design

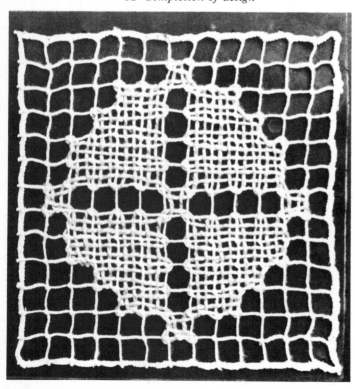

From there the darning process is continued in the other three quarters, though it will be noticed, on Sampler A, that the single projecting squares are not darned and must wait until the thread continues to complete the three horizontal squares and then edges round the whole design, filling in the four outside squares on the way, and finally knotting to the beginning thread.

Other simple shapes, eg 83, 84, and 85, illustrated on a large net for clearness, will give practice in learning this technique. The size of the net will influence their possible use, for pincushion covers (where coloured glass-headed pins, along a line of 'holes' add to the effect), or for lavender sachets, or corners for handkerchiefs, or for tea napkins. Narrow borders could be added to increase the size. The bird, the reindeer, the owl, and the small flower spray make charming little pictures. Some of the diagrams, given later, would also be suitable. A few examples of the use of lacis for table linen, or pillow slips are shown; the butterfly edging was too complicated, it seems, for my 'holes' treatment! The small corner designs on the linen place mats, probably of Italian working, are copied and given separately.

Written descriptive details and diagrams cannot completely teach a technique. When dealing with designs complicated by the existence of many 'holes' a teacher is really needed who uses the correct technique. But any lacis lace-maker will say that much of the pleasure in working it resides in discovering how the design can be followed through. Possibly, in future years, computers will plot the path of the thread for us!

When there was a revival of interest in making this lace in England early in this century unfortunately misleading descriptions were given in some publications and these have been repeated

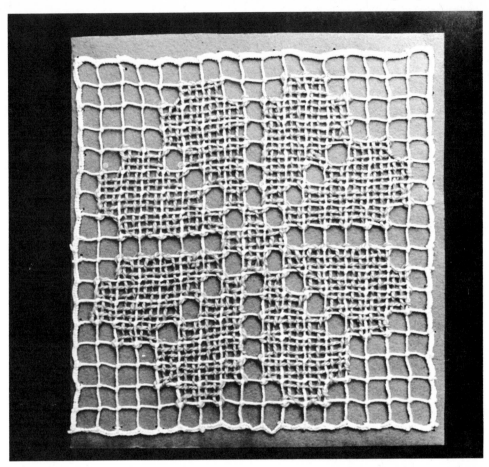

83(a) *Small square — for pincushion etc*   (b) *Shows partly worked square*

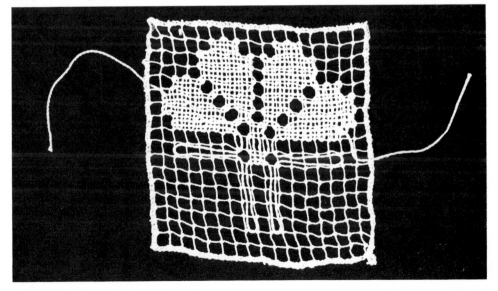

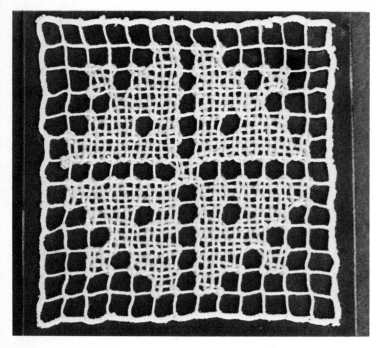

84 Small square

England and on the Continent purporting to teach this old art of lacis I have not come across one that is of real practical value.

I have found so much difficulty in working according to the haphazard, and often incorrect methods adopted by many teachers that I should like to save others from the same experience and at the same time open up to them a new source of interest and occupation.'

Also 'When we sit down with needle and thread we are brought face to face with the fact that the instructions stop short at the point where the first difficulty arises.'

It is my hope to continue her efforts, so that those intending to reproduce some of the old designs on a hand-made knotted net will be willing to follow the early traditional method, and so recapture the joy of using their ingenuity to take the thread along the prearranged pattern that was the designer's intention. They would then share their pleasure with Mary, Queen of Scots and her ladies. In her book *The Needlework of Mary Queen of Scots*[17] Margaret Swain says that ladies were fascinated

since. The author who was most concerned in teaching the correct making of filet lace was 'Carita' (Mrs Simpson) in her book *Lacis*[16]. She was concerned to save people from the problems she herself had experienced. She complained 'Among the books published both in

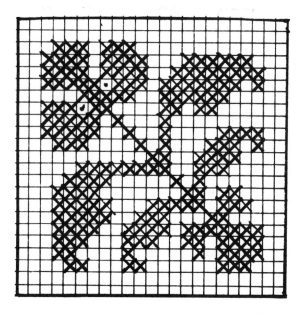

by the intricacies of lacis, and that working out the designs was something of a puzzle, requiring ingenuity and application. 'So it appealed especially to the needlewoman in an age that enjoyed mazes, anagrams and emblems.' She also refers to the often quoted fact that when Mary died, in 1589, nearly 1,000 squares of lacis were said to be found in a box in her possession.

It has proved an exciting experience for the author to use the knowledge of this technique in more difficult pieces of lacis. Some of these may perhaps attract others also to be adventurous (figures 92, 93, 94, 97, 98 and 100).

85 Square could be used as a mat if worked in a large size or if worked in small size could be used as a picture

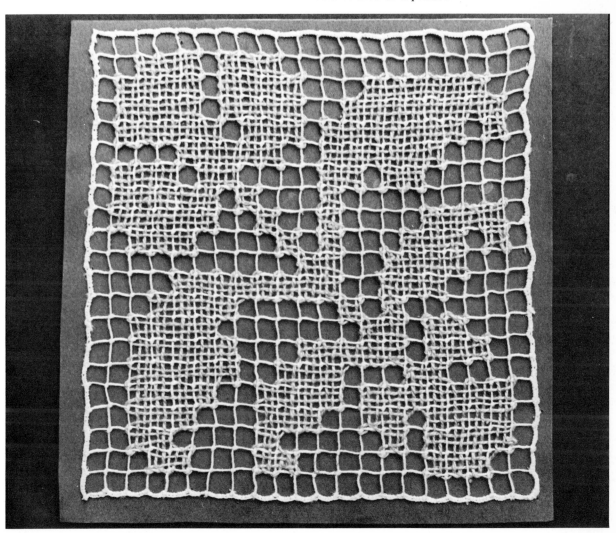

86 Bird – could be used as a picture

*87 Reindeer – could be used in a picture
or as a corner motif*

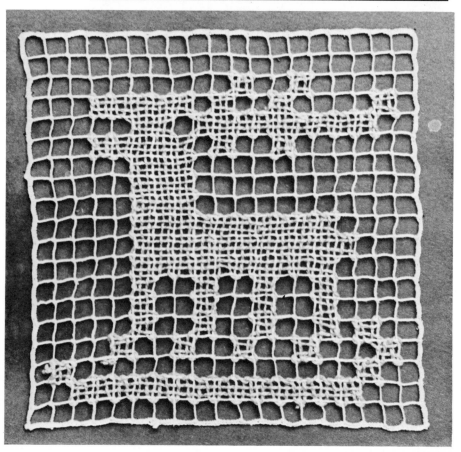

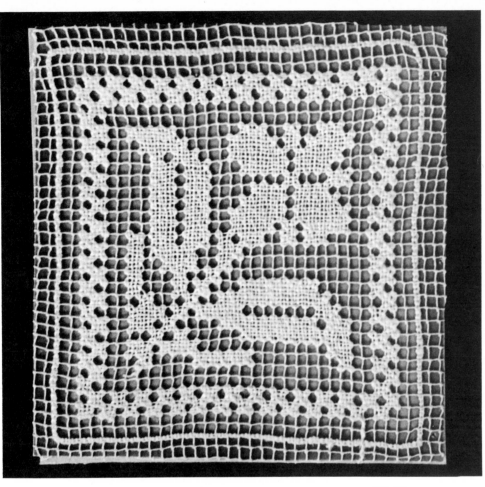

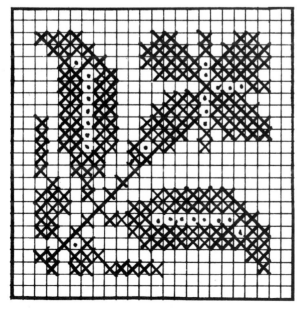

88 Flower spray, could be used in pictures or as corner piece

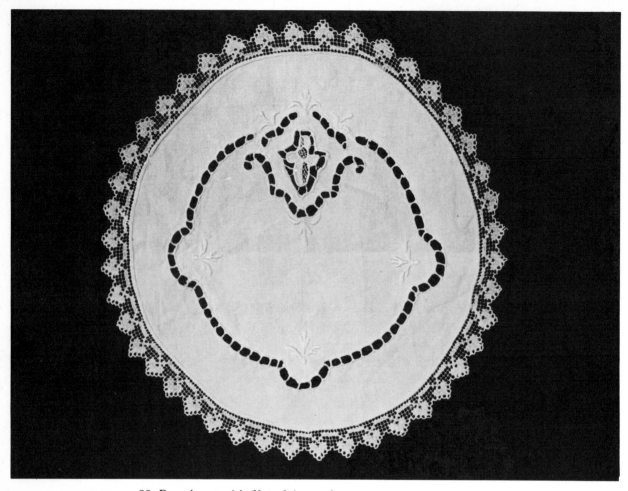

89 *Round mat with filet edging and cut-work embroidery*

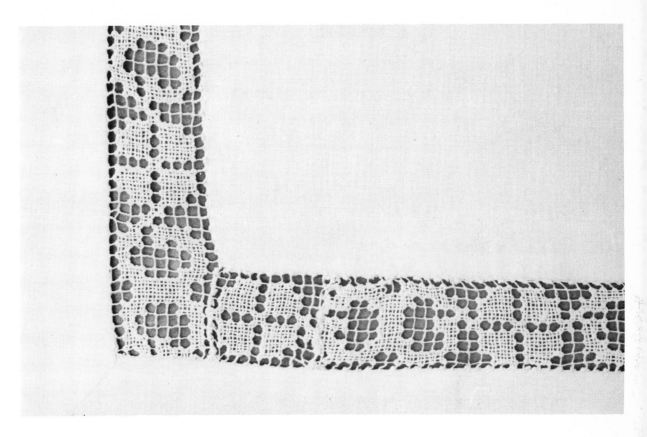

90(a) *Insertion of filet set into a pillow slip*

90(b) *Triangle, one of four, to be set in corners of table linen*

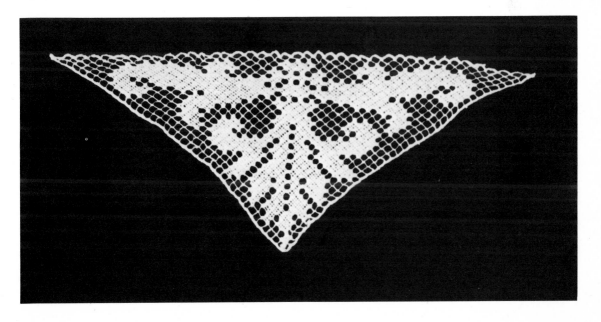

91 *Butterfly edging for table cloth*

92 *Framed picture of two birds*

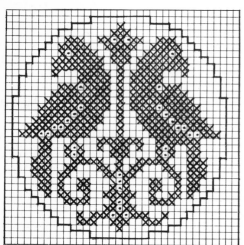

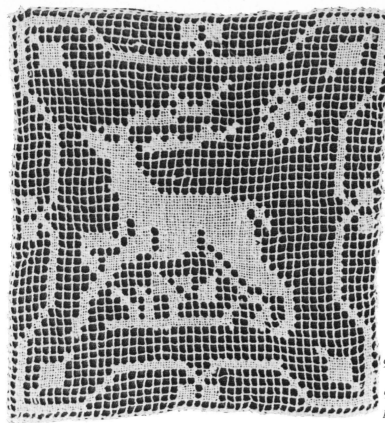

93(a) Running deer, could be framed

93(b) Small stag with tree surround. Key pattern border

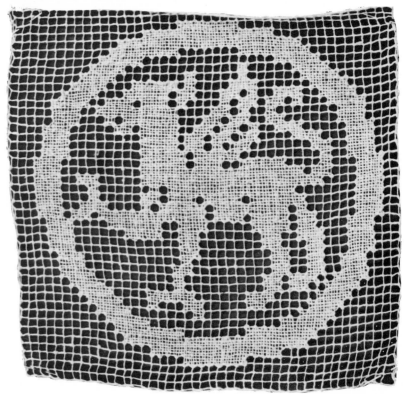

94 *Square with central tree showing facing doves and lions*

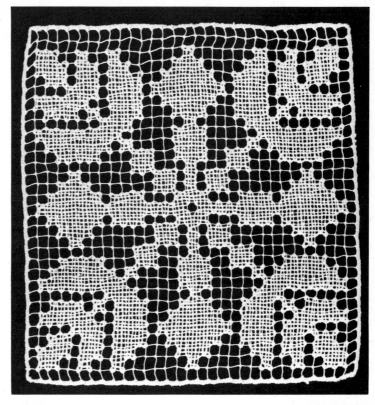

95 *Square with circle enclosing a winged beast*

96 *An elaborate looking mat which is in fact simple to work*

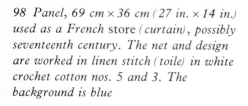

97 *Partly worked mat*

98 *Panel, 69 cm × 36 cm (27 in. × 14 in.)*
used as a French store *(curtain), possibly*
seventeenth century. The net and design
are worked in linen stitch (toile) in white
crochet cotton nos. 5 and 3. The
background is blue

99 *Letters worked in lacis*

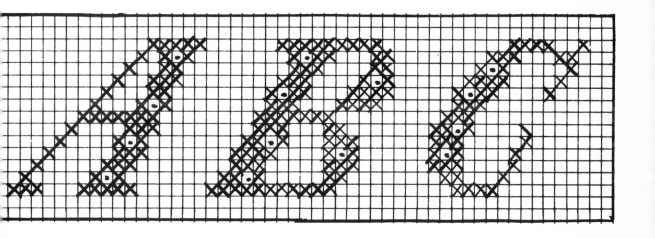

100(a) and 100(b) Two hangings of deer mounted on fawn colour background (152 cm × 254 cm−6 in. × 10 in.)

100(c) Hanging of reindeer, with birds, and trees—from an old design. Try to follow the path of the thread. 33 cm × 34 cm−13 in. × 14 in.

101, 102, 103, 104, 105 Lace mats, prob-
ably Italian, the central designs are
typical of sixteenth century work. The
working of the corners, small animals etc
is shown. Mats are 23 cm (9 in.) square.
Centre square is 14 cm (5½in.) (Courtesy
Mrs Simpson)

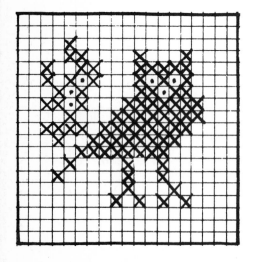

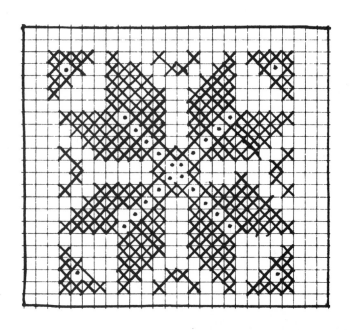

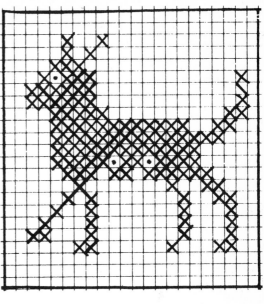

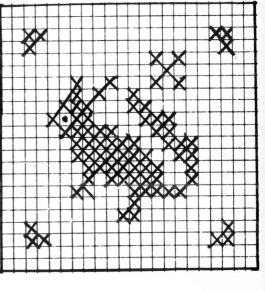

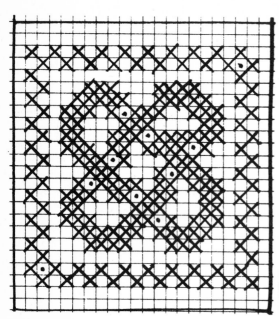

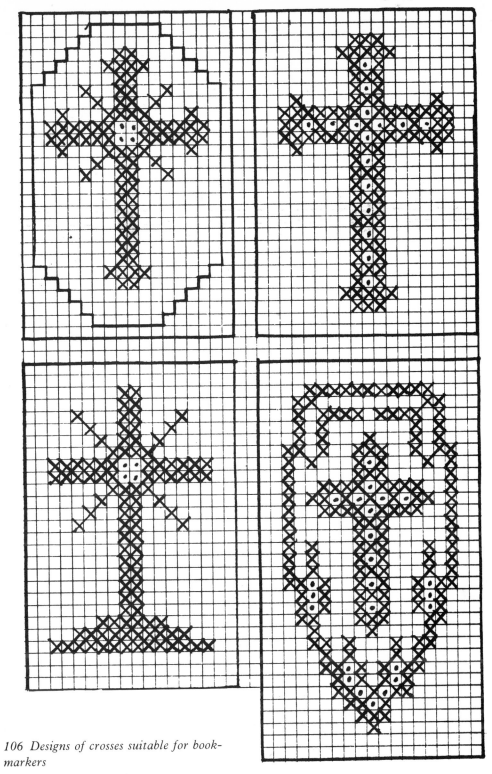

106 *Designs of crosses suitable for book-markers*

107 Pelican and conventional flower
spray (Mrs Purvis's Collection)

108 *Butterflies (Mrs Purvis's Collection)*

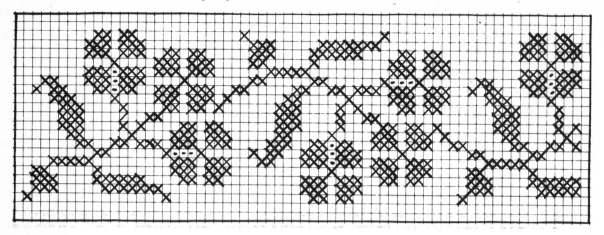

109 *Designs for lace borders or edgings*

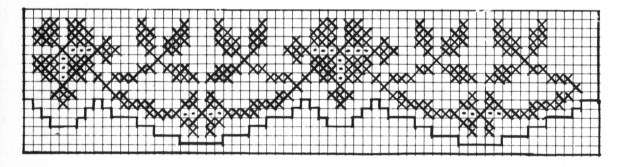

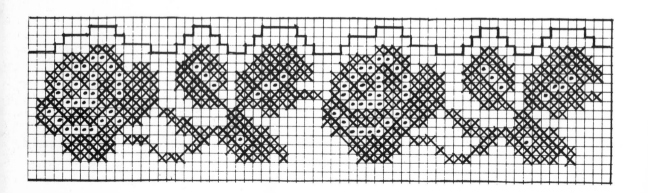

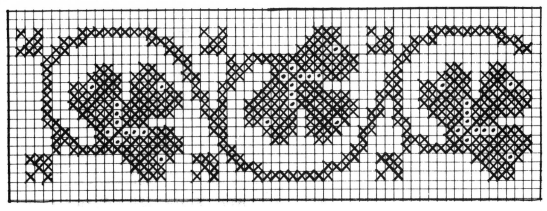

109

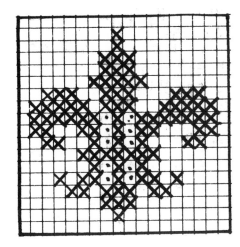

110 *Designs for fleur-de-lis, swan and goose*

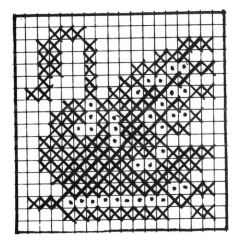

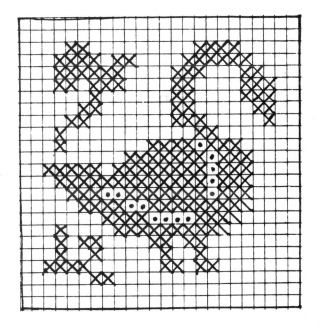

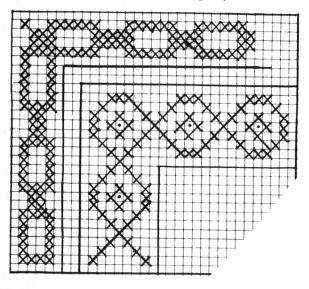

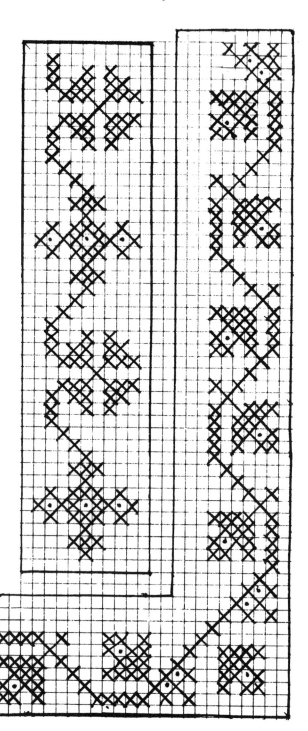

111 Designs of narrow borders to sur-round mats, pictures, or could be used as bookmarkers, doorplates.

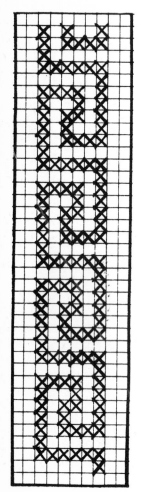

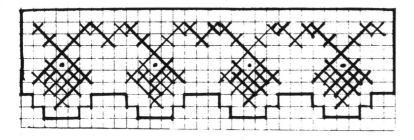

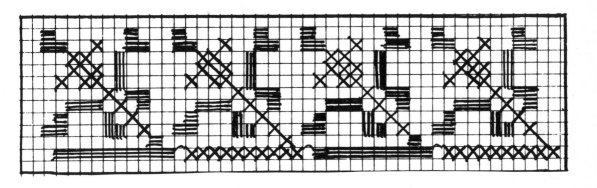

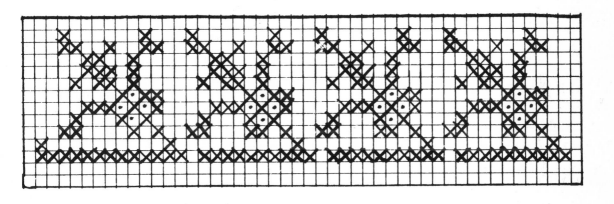

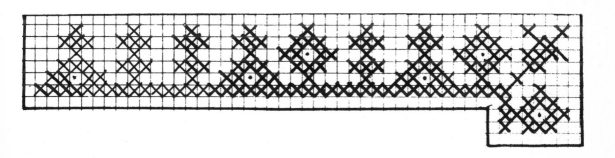

A Victorian Filet Lace Bedspread

A fine specimen of work by two French ladies has been kindly lent to me to help others now to enjoy producing household articles which could be of use for many years and become, perhaps, in their turn, precious heirlooms of the future.

The bedspread, two details of which are shown in figure 112a and b, was prepared as part of her trousseau by my friend's aunt, who worked the exquisite embroiderie Anglaise and cutwork, while her mother made the filet squares and the triangles. This was about seventy years ago and the bedspread has been in use in several tropical parts of the world, yet is still in good condition and a delight to examine in detail. In filet there are actually 144 triangles and 35 squares with a border 1·82 m (2 yd) long at the top and bottom, finished off with a fringe. A narrow bobbin lace ('ninepin') edges the 2·29 m (2½ yd) of its length. A few of the designs have been chosen to give as examples, sometimes with slight alterations, for not all show the continuity which is typical of good filet nor does the worker always use the old method which has been explained.

We do not know whether one particular book of designs was used, or whether they were gradually collected and adapted for this purpose. The frequent appearance of a cross at the centre of a geometric shape suggests an ecclesiastical origin for some parts. As in the best tradition these pieces of lace were varied by the use of others depicting birds and beasts, flowers and leaves.

Squares, figures 113–117, have been worked as examples of these designs and diagrams drafted for them. Diagrams for others, squares and triangles, are given (figures 118 to 121a–k), some quite simple to develop in the correct method (described on pages 68, 69). I should not advise attempting the Griffin without practice in the technique, though he just had to be included!

Each design should be planned with at least one empty row all round. If a square of the exact size needed has been netted that row could be left with its natural double edge. Or, for strengthening it could be buttonholed. If several designs were worked on a large piece of net then the edges to be cut should first have a thread run through them before being buttonholed.

Probably the completion of a whole bedspread seems too daunting a task? Yet squares of such designs as these, with others from old books, or from many published for so-called 'filet-crochet' (which was originally based on the lace) or from cross-stitch designs (where those with a continuous line would be preferable) could be used for

112(a) and overleaf (b) Details from the bedspread

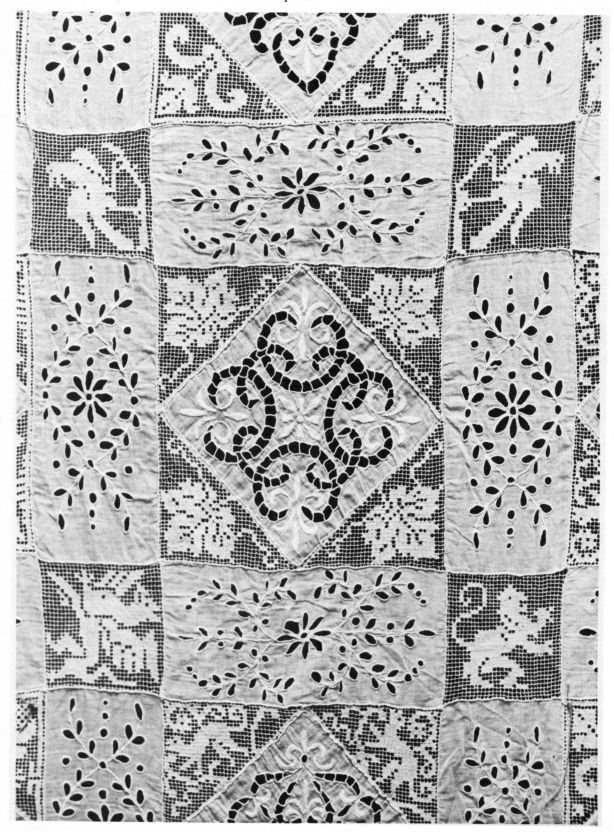

smaller articles. Through the centuries the lace has been used in all household linens, edging or cornering the linen, or as a centre.

For good table linen a linen thread should be used to make the net and the same for the design. The quality of the linen will influence the size of the thread chosen for the design. Linen thread size 40 would suit a fairly heavy linen, and finer numbers for finer materials. Less expensive and giving a different tone would be DMC Cordonnet.

Because some people are attracted to the lace, but delayed in attempting it by the need to be first proficient in making a good piece of net I have contacted several firms for a machine-made, fine filet net. A Nottingham manufacturer makes this (see list of suppliers for retail outlet). It is the same as that used by the lace-makers at the turn of this century. Also it is made by the same process of twisting the threads as was used for the 'sieve' material, for the sixteenth-century Italian buratto lace. Without knots it does not have the true result, and it is not hard wearing. It could be used for practice work, then needing a fine thread.

Some of a larger, machine-made knotted net was obtained and used for mats (figures 76, 77). Further supplies seem doubtful. I am still exploring every avenue to find a source of hand-made net, to order. But it it is not a profitable occupation to undertake, even for institutions for the handicapped.

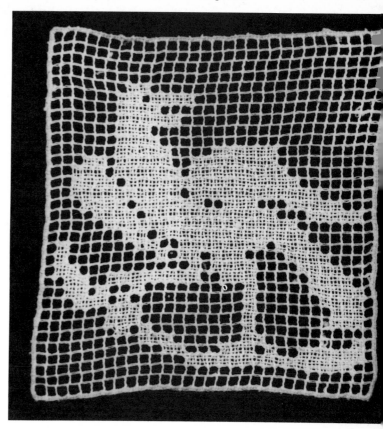

113 Square with eagle

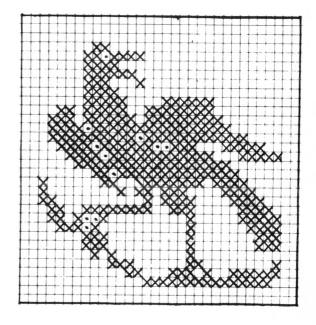

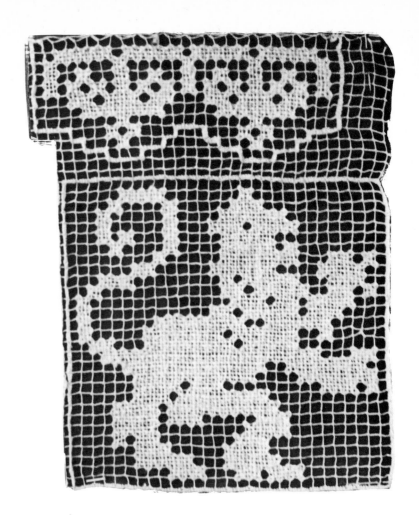

114 Square with lion

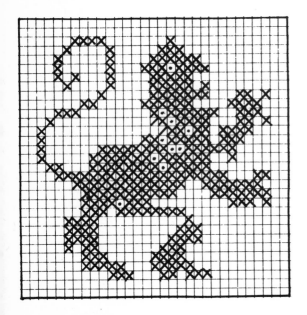

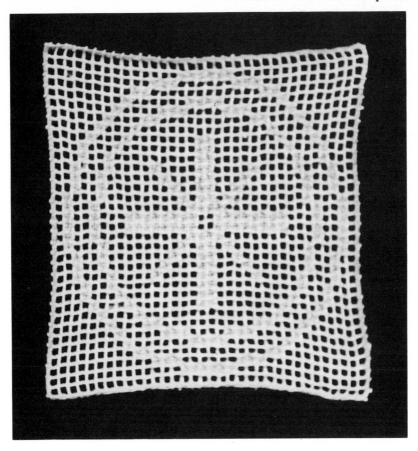

115 Square with cross design within circle

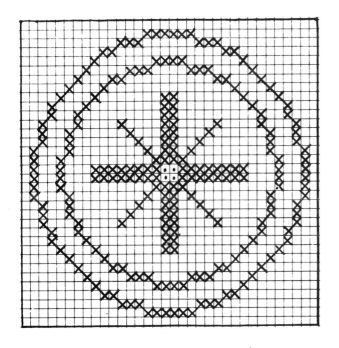

116 *Two squares and a border – the*
border is not part of the bedspread

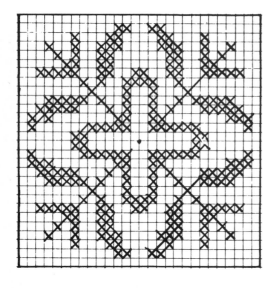

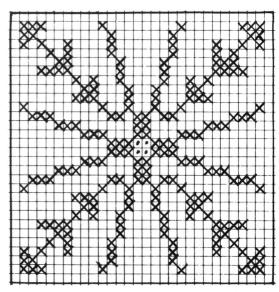

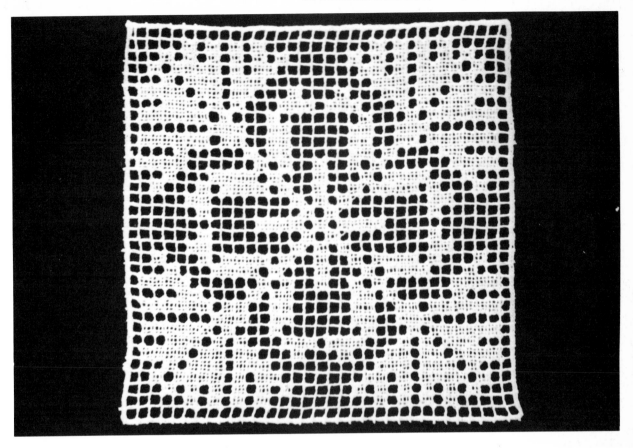

117 Square with carnation design

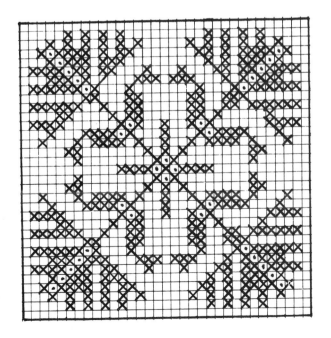

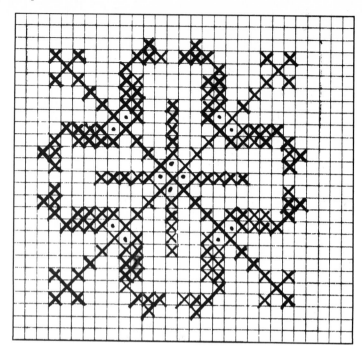

118 Diagrams of squares with cross designs

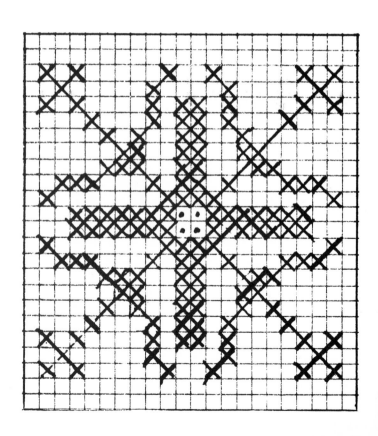

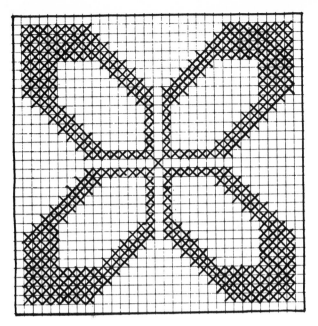

119 Square with geometrical shape

120 Griffin

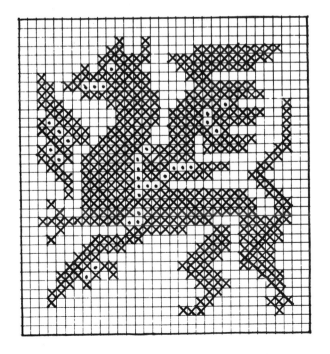

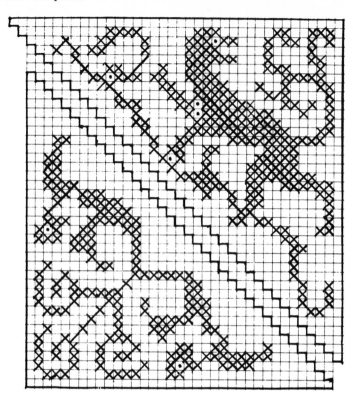

121 *a Monkey*
     b Geometrical shape

c Serpent
d Grapes

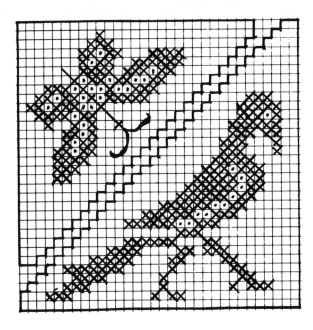

e Butterfly
f Bird

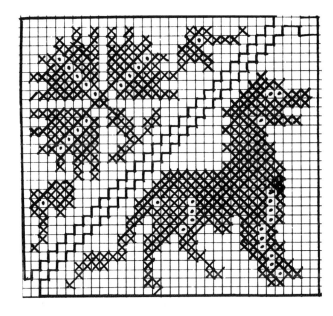

g Carnation
h Dog

i Conventional leaf effects
j Small butterflies
k Small conventional shapes suitable
for napkins, handkerchiefs

Symbolism and Designs

Connected closely with the historical origins and the development of lacis is the interest in the derivation of the designs, and the special meanings associated with them. Certain shapes, such as the cross, the circle, the spiral and the square, with their many derivatives, may be seen in all primitive art and in the earlier known civilisations, accompanied by representations, realistic or emblematic, of animal and human forms. All decorative arts have been derived from basic geometric shapes. Even the twentieth century abstract pictorial art depends on dots, lines and enclosed spaces; the formulation of these into definite shapes appears to satisfy some innate human impulse. Also the natural forms of plant life, the distinctive appearances of different trees, flowers, leaves and fruits are used in all their varieties to beautify objects of purely utilitarian value.

Now that modern science, with electron microscopes, has revealed to us the infinite complexity of the molecules, as in the double helix DNA, we may come to realise that 'design' is of the essential nature of the universe. So we delight the more in seeing and reproducing some small part of it in a creative act. Who has not studied with intense admiration drawings of the snow crystals? Mr Horning's book[18] gives no less than 81 pictures of their designs, shown alternately on white and dark backgrounds. In the notes on the plates he states that the snow-crystal is one of the most exciting demonstrations of the universal law of geometry, and speaks of the infinity of designs which are revealed by a minute study of their crystalline forms from the basic six radii. To an artist with her needle they could be the inspiration for hangings, mobiles, delicate bridal veils, or dress collars, in netting or other laces.

It is interesting that in considering the earliest dates for lacework Mrs Hungerford Pollen[19] stresses the early geometric character of primitive designs. She finds the inspiration for these in Eastern influences, especially in Coptic art of the first to third centuries, where the simplicity of the forms used had for them the deeper meanings of the Christian faith.

There is also reference in Mrs Averil Colby's book[20] to the influence of the Near East in the Egyptian patterns, geometrical in character, found on textiles in burial grounds. One sampler she describes as of Coptic work, probably of the fifth century, which showed Christian emblems, in darning stitch, worked in red, blue, green and brown wools.

One such emblem is that of the Greek cross formed of the capital gammas all facing outward so that the ends of the arms of the cross are open (a).

These signs have been found on the

a

b

walls of the catacombs where Christians had met to worship secretly. The shape of (b), with its possible suggestion of an emblem of the Sun Wheel was used as a disguised cross, and so called the *crux dissimulata* and the *crux gammata*. A mystic symbol of such ancient use (it was known in India 3 000 years before Christ) might have expressed for them its Sanskrit derivation of 'it is well' and 'so be it', or their trust in the ultimate power of God.

In the thirteenth century the swastika shape became associated with St Francis, possibly, suggests Mrs Hungerford Pollen,[21] because the gammadion was worked among a variety of polygonal forms on the Assisi alb, said to have been worn by him.

On Plate III of her book is a photograph of a detail of the alb (figure 122) with the gammadion, or early Christian symbol.

Her interpretation of the symbolism underlying such designs is that of the idea of evolution, of mysteries turning and repeating themselves indefinitely. Figure 123 is described as an interesting border of Sicilian lacis, the design Eastern, introducing the gammadion, the netting all made obliquely.

When adopted in European art the swastika appeared in such embroideries as altar cloths and curtains. Examples of these are among the plates in that valuable volume for the study of European needlework, *The Art of Embroidery*[22] by Marie Schuette and Sigrid Müller-Christensen.

In another altar curtain of the mid-thirteenth century, in the innumerable squares of complicated geometrical designs appears a variety of the swastikas. Other cloths and curtains of the twelfth to the fourteenth century reveal the delight of designers and embroiderers in spirals, scrolls and floral motifs within circles, lozenges or hexagonal shapes with backgrounds of truly involved geometrical patterns. For them there would still have been religious significance in these shapes used as the background to the Biblical scenes depicted.

It is not suggested that the symbolic ideas originally expressed in so many formal decorative arts remained in the minds of all those later using and developing them. It is almost axiomatic that emblems once expressing religious, tribal and national ideas lose these significances yet keep something of their influence.

Mrs Averil Colby[23] notices how a basic tradition persists in the planning of samplers and the flower, animal and human forms used in the embroidery through several centuries.

Her comment is 'it seems one could look even further than a traditional use of some patterns which occur from the sixteenth century onwards and a possible explanation may lie in a deeply rooted but unconscious attachment to symbolic forms, to which embroiderers had become accustomed in ecclestiastical and heraldic work'.

This is especially noticeable if we refer again to early Christian symbols and their use in lace making. It was in the convents and monasteries of the medieval period that both men and women designed and produced all the articles in church use, for the altar, all its furnishings, the cloths and veils and the priests' ceremonial robes, especially for the higher dignitaries. It is recorded that St Dunstan designed patterns for the Anglo-Saxon ladies who were skilled with their needle. The embroidery of English nuns became famous throughout Europe and was known as *opus Anglicanum*. English kings sent these embroidered copes to

122 Detail of the Assisi alb

123 Lacis with gammadion, fifteenth century, Italian

the Popes, who themselves commissioned such work for Italian churches. It is the description of the details of this work which is of importance for our consideration of lace designs.

In *The Art of Embroidery*[24] the authors speak of 'the progressive modification and enrichment of the composition, from the earlier pieces with subjects in circles, eight-pointed stars and quatrefoils, to the later ones in which Gothic arches form tabernacles for the figures of the saints. The intervals are filled with flowering scrolls and a multitude of birds, beasts and horses unparalleled elsewhere'. Such examples as the Syon cope and the Grandison altar frontal of the late thirteenth century are well-known, while innumerable other embroideries are still in a good state of preservation. These are always the large pieces, tapestries, altar furnishings and curtains and vest-

ments. But other articles were in daily use during church services.

The albs and surplices worn by the priests were also ornamented, while the linen work of chalice veils, corporals and towels gave other opportunities for delicate stitchery. It is understandable that these latter were more perishable, especially because of the need for laundering. Yet the loose even weave of linen is the ideal ground for drawn-thread and cut-work which some would claim as the origin of lace forms.

One example of white-work illustrated in *The Art of Embroidery* is the Lenten altar cloth from Lower Saxony of the late thirteenth century. It is described as 'linen ground with drawn thread work with darned patterns'. It shows a net-like ground on which are worked various cross and star shapes between the figures representing Pilate and soldiers.

For ecclesiastical purposes the most frequently used designs were naturally developments of the cross, with other symbols which had come to be connected with the lives of saints. It seems that the swastika did not remain as long in use in lace work as in the tapestries. But the basic two lines, crossing at right angles, became *the* sacred sign of Christianity. It was adopted by ruling families and in innumerable societies and commercial life (eg stone-masons) throughout the Western world, possibly still with some aura of its pre-Christian association of spiritual life and power.

Is it generally realised how potent was the symbol of the cross to the people of the Minoan civilisation in Crete, about 2000 BC? All its various forms existed there, not just as purely ornamental designs but with a profoundly mystical significance.

The Aegean Civilisation[25] by Gustave Glotz reveals the fascinating story of their lives, art and religion at the time when they were masters of the Mediterranean, trading with Cyprus and Egypt to the East and as far as Spain in the West.

It was the tau cross shape familiar to the English as that of St George, which St Olaf, in 1030, ordered his sons to paint on their shields before their fight with the pagan Scandinavians.

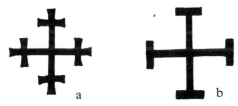

a   b

When Pope Urban II in 1095 proclaimed the First Crusade he told the soldiers 'The Cross of Christ is the symbol of your salvation'. Later, with differing colours, it was used to distinguish the separate armies, on shields, banners and badges of all the Crusaders, and then of the noblemen and their retainers. Hence the art of Heraldry, and also its influence upon lace designs.

It is natural that for embroiderers, especially those working on an even foundation of squares, such as net, the formal lines of cross patterns gave ample opportunity for experimenting with variations and embellishments. (Figures 111, 115 and 118.)

In many designs of filet lace can be traced the Cross potent made up of four Tau crosses joined at the centre (a), and the Cross-crosslet of four Latin crosses similarly joined (b).

Surrounded by a circle there would be the additional symbol of eternity, without beginning or end (figure 115). Within a square it would include the many ideas connected with four – evangelists, elements, compass points etc – and the rightness (four right angles) seen in the modern colloquial use of 'four square' and 'fair and square'. We do not realise how often familiar phrases contain depths of meaning.

Hexagonal and octagonal shapes may enclose large or small crosses, often with lines radiating, to extend, as it were, the power from the centre (figures 111 and 116).

Because of the use on Crusaders' shields, the Latin cross, with the longer vertical lines, was frequently used in Heraldry and in lace designing. When the shields were shortened, crosses with arms of nearly equal length resulted again. Forms where the arms terminate into points (c) or splay into three curves (d) are in heraldry known at Patonce and Flory. They break the rigidity of straight lines, adding ornamental effect, while the three curves of the flory suggest the fleur-de-lis, with its reference to the Trinity.

The quite different, well-known Maltese cross of the Knights of St John (e) seems to be less used in lacis: its sharply pointed shape would not suit a squared ground.

c

d

e

There are many other variants lending themselves to decorative treatments.
Often for lace there might be a squared
centre, solid or left open. Seldom seen
is that of Calvary, with the steps. Yet it,
with others described, if worked in a
white or gold-coloured thread are most
suitable, applied to braids, for use as
bookmarkers. (Figure 111.)

As edgings for linen cloths there can
be used a simple repetition of one of the
cross designs, as is seen in crochet patterns suggested for Church use. But this
would not occur in old lace: for the
main designs would not be isolated.
True, a variety of cross and star and
other shapes were dotted around the
chief figures over the back of a seated
stag (figure 47), and in any empty sky
spaces, even into already closely packed
designs. Figure 46 depicts, as well as
small trees and a bird in odd corners
about *ten* little 'angular angels' surrounding the 'glory of flames' which
enclose an octagon to contain the sacred
monogram I H S.[26]

In this avoidance of empty spaces not
only crosses but all possible star patterns were used, still at times with a
symbolic intention or just its vague
remembrance. The five-pointed star, the
pentagram, had many interpretations, in
true mysticism and also in occult, magi-
cal practices and so was used as an
amulet.

The hexagon as a six-pointed star
does seem to suggest to us the idea of a
star in the heavens. Also it is the pattern on which various crystals are made;
and it appears so often in flower for-
mations that it naturally appeals to the
designer. The Seal of Solomon, the
view of the hexagon as the interlacing of
two equilateral triangles has special
meanings in Hebrew history and is
known as the Star of David (a). It
makes an interestingly beautiful new
symmetrical pattern with the six small

distinct triangles grouped round a central hexagon. Again it might have been
associated with all the divine conno-
tations surrounding the lily family,
through the flowering herb known as
Solomon's Seal.

It seems that the earliest examples of
lacis reveal the fascination of geometric
shapes for the designers. The influence
remains, in embroideries also, in the
separating of figures by polygonal
enclosures or within pointed arcadings,
often of architectural origin.

There are many examples of this in
The Art of Embroidery[27] eg the detail
shown of the St Andrew cope of the
early fourteenth century. And there is a
charming small picture reproduced in
Barbara Snook's book[28] of a panel of
the Adoration of the Magi.

These cross references between lace
and embroidery designs seem necessary
when so little remains of the early lace
work. Yet while their companions were
dedicated to the production of such
great work as the copes of the *opus
Anglicanum* one cannot imagine that
the nuns concerned with less grand
items, for liturgical use, would be less
ambitious in their zeal for representing
symbols of the faith in the details of
their designs.

Those symbols included not only the
geometric shapes and the cruciform
variations but also, with increasing
interest, the plant forms of the natural
world and often the unnatural life
portrayed.

Why was it that the lily flower
became of such religious significance?
We are familiar with its association with
the Virgin Mary, through the pictures
of the Annunciation, where the Angel
Gabriel sometimes held the flowers in
his hand, or where they were planted in
a pot near her. Repeated variations of
the scene used a stylised vase of flowers,
not necessarily lilies. Yet the virtues

a

attributed to Mary of purity and humility remained attached to the flower, while its trefoil petals received another symbol of the Trinity. There may even have been earlier, pre-Christian influence persisting, which surfaced again, from the Indian lotus and the Egyptian waterlily.

Many centuries later, by Louis VII of France in the twelfth century, there was adopted, on a seal, a single fleur-de-lis as an emblem of royalty, with a legendary religious connection with Clovis, King of the Franks.

In embroidery and lace designs the form which persisted for many years to have a religious significance was the pot with flowers, natural or conventionalised. It is one of the designs given in 1605 in an Anglo-French pattern book for lacis – *La Pratique de L'Aiguille Industrieuse* by M. Matthias Mignerack. The well-known book *Pillow Lace*[29] by Mincoff and Marriage has this reference to it: 'For the most part it contains patterns for darned net, remarkable for their methodical arrangement and strange subjects. The author seems to have had in mind the construction of some great coverlid in squares, some with flower-pots. The scenes are most ambitious, representing Danae with the shower of gold, Lucretia piercing her breast, the elements, the seasons, "La Charité Romaine" and other curious pictures.' Those were the designs so eagerly translated into lace articles and hangings, and later printed to amaze us in nineteenth century publications.

In such lace pieces the pot might be an attractive vase, or just a narrow base from which flowers sprayed out: there were innumerable variations. Its appeal as a design for needlework remained popular long after any symbolic idea had been forgotten. It was accepted as an essential part of a sampler, often being repeated for different stitchery treatment. Perhaps even the branching stems separating pairs of birds and animals may be a vague recurrence, when not intended as an actual tree-like form.

Sometimes the flower rose high above the vase in scrolls with flowers and leaves as offshoots. There is an illustration of this in Plate 99 of *The Art of Embroidery*,[30] depicting a side panel of the Grandison Altar Frontal attributed to English workers of about 1300. Alternating scolls at each side of a central stem from the pot lift up (through 88 cm –34 in.) beautiful branches with vine leaves, grapes, and spiralling tendrils, curving into scrolls as those on the pot. This type of design occurred so often that examples were reproduced for lacis in the French Albums in the nineteenth century. There is a certain satisfaction in its formal beauty of line, and it became a favourite design type for French curtains ('stores').

The Grandison altar frontal introduces yet another symbolic plant, the vine. This seems to be the one most often reproduced in filet. It is amazing how, on the squared ground of net, leaves and branches can be shaped into beautiful curving lines, with a symmetry in placing them to balance the scrolls, when repeated along lace edges or coiled round circles, squares, etc. From the samples I have seen of Italian Buratto lace of the sixteenth and seventeenth centuries these designs seemed specially favoured there (figures 36 to 38). The ground material used, however, was not that of a knotted net, but a loosely woven linen on which the leaves were usually worked in toile (linen stitch). The curious curved lines extending into circles from some points of the leaves on these, and on other vine designs, bring to mind some of the illuminated manuscripts of the same periods.

Those who prepared the many designs of vine leaves and grapes, and the nuns who reproduced them on linen and on the knotted net had joy in their knowledge of the mystic significance. The grapes spoke to them of the wine sanctified in its use at the Eucharist, the symbol of Jesus applied to himself, with its further reference to the Church and Christ as the Keeper of the Vineyard.

Then, perhaps, the more general thought came suggested by the Old Testament, 'But they shall sit everyman under his vine and under his fig tree; and none shall make them afraid'–the picture of peace and plenty. Why not, too, as they saw its preparation around them, the anticipation of 'wine that maketh glad the heart of man'?

Associating the fig-tree with the vine could recall that it represented fruitfulness and good works, while yet reminding them of other, evil aspects of fertility, and of the Tree of Knowledge of the Garden of Eden: for that was sometimes described as the fig tree, not the apple.

Another plant, reproduced usually to show its many seeds, is the pomegranate, for so long, and in so many countries a decorative emblem. From forms simulating the actual fruit there developed stylized motifs we would hardly recognise as the fruit. Again the many seeds spoke of fertility with also a deeper aspect, of eternity.

So there could be a wealth of meaning for each separate fruit, flower and tree as well as in a combination of some together. The strawberry, representing the righteousness of the Virgin and good works, joined with the violet in its humility, gave the thought that the spiritual and righteous are truly humble.

The so frequent appearance of a formal carnation flower had puzzled me for any figurative idea, though its attractiveness can be seen (figure 117). Among these symbols suggested is that of 'pure love', later 'motherly love' and so of 'fidelity and marriage'. The nail-shaped clove recalled the Crucifixion.

Any three-petalled or three-leaved plant, eg the clover (shamrock), the strawberry, the trefoils, spoke of the Trinity. For the Holy Spirit the Columbine was the flower emblem, connected with the bird-like florets giving a likeness to the dove (Latin – Columba). And the Dove is the accepted symbol of the Spirit.

It was associated also with the story of the Flood, as it returned to the Ark, bearing the olive leaf. Thus it became a symbol of peace. We have seen it too, in many lacis designs, near to or drinking from a fountain, as being nourished at the Fountain of Life. Even without a religious connotation it keeps, in our imaginations, something of gentleness and innocence.

> *Oh, no man knows*
> *Through what wild centuries*
> *Roves back the rose.*[31]

A decided fondness for gardens and flowers is a generally accepted characteristic of English people, with the special love for the rose. The image of the simple wild rose holds something of the nostalgia felt for the beauty and peace of the countryside – as in Rupert Brooke's recollections of Grantchester –

> *Unkempt about those hedges blows*
> *An English unofficial rose.*

Alas: there are few of those unkempt hedges now, for the wild rose to flourish there.

It was that wild flower which became the national floral emblem, with its five fully-opened petals, the barbs between to represent the calyx, and the stamens or seeds in a small central circle.

Its appearance on a badge of Edward

I, possibly in memory of his mother, Eleanor of Provence, offers us another tradition to connect it with a religious background and significance. For it was said to have been introduced into Provence by the returning Crusaders.

When the rival houses of York and Lancaster, whose badges were the white and red roses, combined these to produce the Tudor Rose, with the marriage of Elizabeth of York to Henry of Lancaster, we see yet another symbol of royalty, with that of reconciliation and peace.

In the vandyke border of lacis (figure 53) can be seen a similarity to the Tudor Rose, though not with the five petals. Many later designs, especially those adopted in the last century, attempted to present realistic rose shapes; these are difficult to work by the correct method, because of the irregularity of the 'holes'. Most of the rose's special meanings in Christian art are concerned with Mary, recalling in the use of the rosary the joyful and the sorrowful mysteries of her life.

More frequently when used in lace designs, they were conventionalized, and rose shapes were joined into garlands surrounding figures, or separating other designs, or as borders around the whole piece, or enclosed beautifully into circular and hexagonal figures.

Tudor Rose

On the military standard of the Roman soldiers was carried the emblem of an eagle. Thus one recalls that the eagle was the special bird of Jupiter (Jove) the supreme Roman deity, especially in his role as protector in battle.

That has been the symbol most accepted for the innumerable examples of the representations of the bird, in Europe. At his coronation in Rome in 800 AD Charlemagne is said to have adopted the eagle as his ensign, with the claim to be a successor of the Roman Emperor. It was then depicted with the wings raised on each side of the upright body, head turning to the right or the left, and the legs stretched out with the tail between them. A strange picture! Yet the one which persisted, even later, when by Frederic Barbarossa, crowned in 1155, it became the recognised standard of the Holy Roman Empire. Afterwards the even stranger double-headed eagle (whose origin has been suggested as designed when two princes ruled together, or as possibly Turkish) was seen on seals of the King of Poland (1255) of the Emperor Sigismund (1314), later on the arms of Austria and of Russia, with varying additions in its heraldic appearances.

It is not surprising, therefore, that we find this strange bird shown, in lace work, not only standing aloft (figure 6) or with wings spread (figure 124) but on a variety of designs associated with all the European countries, though only occasionally in Britain. It is there always as a royal emblem of authority and power, often combined with an attitude of fierceness.

A bird which offered delightful possibilities of displaying the designer's art and the lacemaker's skill is the peacock. It may strut along proudly trailing its long tail: or full face 'in its pride' raise the brilliant many-eyed circle of feathers above and around it. With several legends talking of its flesh as incorruptible and of the feathers being renewed each spring it symbolised resurrection as well as its obvious worldly pride (figure 46).

As symbols of resurrection two other birds are represented, the pelican and the phoenix. The former has another attribute, that of protective care for the young, shown as the blood from her breast, pierced by her beak, nourishes the fledglings in the nest below her. This is the design given in Vinciolo's book,[32] which would have been worked in the reprise stitch. In lace work I have not yet found any such figure given, only the very long beak of the bird which might suggest the well-known tale. Figure 107 shows a different poise, flying downwards.

However, in a copy of the book *A*

124 Eagle worked in linen stitch

Scholehouse for the Needle[33] seen in the Library of the Victoria and Albert Museum, there were several different Pelican designs given (not on a squared ground).

A much less spectacular bird than these two – the owl – is familiarly called 'the wise old owl' because of its associa-tion with Minerva, the goddess of Wisdom. In both lacework and heraldry the bird is shown with the head facing forward but the body to the side and wings closed. So the large eyes are emphasised. The small owl seen in figure 126 is worked in a two-tone thread of white and light brown which suggested the colouring and texture of feathers: it was framed as a pleasant

125 Typical strange bird design with small, quaint creatures

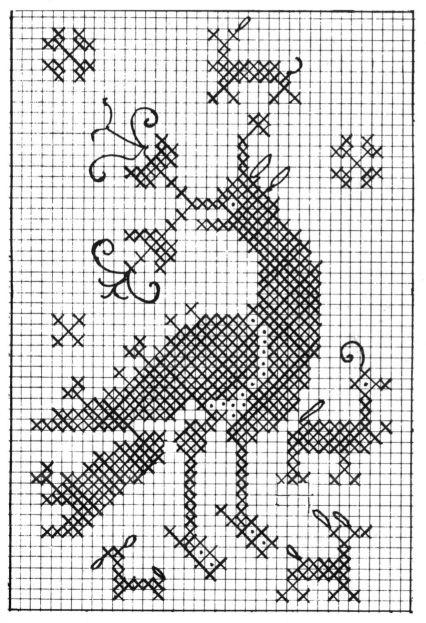

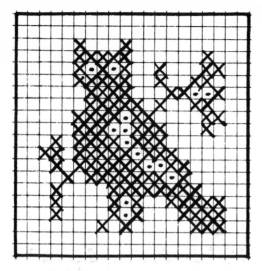

126 Owl diagram

little picture. Other examples (figures 132 and 133) also show it always depicted full-face forward.

Small birds of various sizes and of no definitely discernible species will be found in any spaces which the designer did not want to leave empty. It is amusing to examine the slight differences in stance that are presented with an ingenuity in placing them among the main figures.

Among the designs drawn in *The Scholehouse for the Needle* there were some delightful natural studies of recognisable birds. Usually there were two, facing, with some trees branching between them, or they were retreating from each other into an intricate pattern of foliage.

Yet in so many of the designs presented in the nineteenth century French Albums and in other Needlework Journals the birds seem chosen for their unusual or even fantastic appearance. Of course, they therefore attract our attention and set us imagining the pictures to be prepared by working them.

Quite different were the associations, in the thoughts of the convent workers, concerned with the dove, as representing the Holy Spirit. Usually it is depicted as flying downwards, with wings outspread, within a circle or octagon of radiating lines and so described as 'set in glory'. It is interesting to see that such an interpretation in embroidery used alternating straight and waved lines.

So often, in lacis, there is the theme introduced of Birds at a Fountain, again one that is used in other artistic media, to represent eternal life.

It must be remembered that lacework is not as suitable a medium for large heavy hangings as were the tapestries and embroideries. Within their usually narrower limits the designers formed trees in curvilinear meanderings from which coiled branches with leaves and blossoms: so there was the continuing symbol of recurrence, abundance and strength. (Figures 24 to 27.)

Where woodland scenes were suggested it would be at the lower level, which contained the hunters and animals of the chase – a favourite subject; while in early designs a full-grown tree might be of the same height as an animal near it, in no way in proportion. Realism was not an essential element of their designs. Nor may every scene or separate tree, flower and fruit always be planned with a symbolical content. We need to use some caution when attributing deliberately hidden meanings to what were pictorial art forms, especially in England, after the Reformation when we are concerned with work from the Elizabethan age onwards. For then lace was used to decorate every possible part of the dress of men and women, even – for men – as flounces edging breeches and top boots. Think of the pictures of the Cavaliers!

With that warning in mind we may continue to discuss designs with the thought of special meanings given to them in earlier work.

We have already seen the importance of representations of the grapes for the Eucharistic Wine. So the branching vine would be the most frequently repeated design, in many variations, for articles prepared for use at the altars, the fair linen cloth, the corporal and burse, the paten cover, and the towel.

The two borders of darned netting (figures 26, 27) show differing treatments of the conventional vine stem. The first design is worked completely in toile, introducing two variants of the leaf, rather solidly worked. A lighter effect is introduced in the arcading chain, with its tiny cross-tipped motifs, and the odd 'crook', and other small motifs in any spare space.

In the border in figure 27 the leaves are much more elaborate in their shape, deeply lobed, with leaf tips curving upwards. There is a subtle use of the two stitches, toile and reprise to give a delightful shading. In the arcading also both stitches are used. An amusing addition is a tiny bird, in each division, tasting the juice of the bunch of grapes.

In the exuberant design shown in figure 127 there can be interest and amusement in trying to decide exactly which leaves, flowers and fruits the artist had prepared for the lacemaker, and what, if any, symbolism was expressed in it, probably in the sixteenth century. To examine the stitchery in detail is to see the delightful effects achieved by the use of the two stitches, with the addition of terminating scrolls, small hooks and an unusual open-work centre (pulled stitch) to what may be pomegranates.

The curves of the branching which divide the design repeats are unevenly broken, crossed by the leaf stalks, and at one side joined by a narrow ribbon-scroll. The leafy border shapes, with hook ends at the tips, are again worked in both stitches. They give a more formal, usual, effect by their regular repetition, so perhaps moderating the extravagance of the whole design.

In the nineteenth century albums and journals, with the revival of interest in filet lace, there was given an abundant choice of vine patterns, less ambitious than the above, for the new lacemakers. Still, in Christian churches of most denominations crochet patterns of vine leaves and grapes are used to imitate the old lace, continuing its devotional intent. In fact it saddened me, when visiting cathedrals and churches in Northern France, to find only crochet, not the true laces, commonly in use there.

Not only the leaf of the vine but also the tendrils attracted the medieval designers, who often curled them into spiral forms. Also delicate trails of ivy leaves were a favourite ornamentation of the bars surrounding the texts in illuminated manuscripts, English and French, in the fourteenth and fifteenth centuries. The several lobes of the acanthus, and of fig leaves with their clearly marked veinings were used by all artists for decoration. So they appear in lace designs whether in a conventionalised shape or naturally attempted. So also one finds oak leaves and acorns and various other leaves and fruits, whether composing the main design, or as additional motifs.

English designers in all forms of artistic endeavours appear to have had special delight in using their observations of nature and enlivening them with imaginative additions.

We can learn more about the sources for illuminators, painters, embroiderers and lace and tapestry-makers. We remember that designers were employed in courts and by noble families to provide the patterns. They set up workshops which were responsible for some of the excellent, as well as the inferior work developed. They travelled around

the Continent; so it is not surprising that similar designs were repeated in all the varieties of artistic products and that it is often difficult to be definite about the country of origin of lace still remaining, or of its date, as the same designs continued to be used for years later.

The Bestiaries of the twelfth and thirteenth centuries appear to have provided the following centuries with the fabulous creatures they delighted to depict.

They also provided the horrific beasts so many of whom may also now be seen in their splendour of gorgeous colours in books on Heraldry. Apart from the recognisable lions, and leopards, there appear unicorns, scaly dragons, griffins (or gryphons), chimeras – with gaping jaws, some winged and fiercely claw-footed, or with long serpent-like tails. To read the descriptions of these hybrid monsters is to marvel what strange imaginings could have conceived them. Where can we still see them represented? – as the gargoyles perched on cathedral roofs or in stone carvings surmounting capitals within the walls! They are usually considered to have had an Eastern origin.

One recalls television programmes and the dinosaurs who populated our earth for so many millions of years. A recently-discovered fossil, possibly of the first part-winged part-reptile animal, when 'rebuilt' bore a strong resemblance to these beasts used for so many designs.

If an awareness of these strange beings came from the East how did they become accepted to be used by medieval artists as true descriptions of to them unknown animals? The usual

response is to refer to the tales brought back by the Crusaders and to ideas that there might have been confusions with accounts of actual animals, eg of the unicorn with the narwhal or the rhinoceros.

In his book *The Etruscans*[34] Werner Keller suggests that there persisted into the Roman period and the early centuries of Christianity the influences of the Etruscan civilisation of the seventh century BC. For their tombs were known, where on the walls and on pottery and bronze vessels there were representations of lions, panthers, leopards and ostriches, as well as of the strange chimeras, sphinxes and griffins from the near East. Such figures were included in churches in parts of Italy and hence came not only the gargoyles but also their influence on the imagination and artistic life, especially in the monasteries and convents.

Perhaps this will help us to understand now, the fascination for embroiderers and lacemakers of the fantastic animals included in their designs.

To compare them, however, with their counterparts in heraldic pictures is to realise that in the usual white-work of lacis they become much less horrific. Personally I have quite a liking for the little lions around the borders of figures 43 and 44 and the many 'rampant' lions (figure 114) or nobly 'supporting' a shield, or facing each other across spreading flowers (figure 31). An idea of power has been associated with them, from their Eastern lands. There were lions around Solomon's throne and their attributes are that of guarding and protecting. It is interesting how the two lions expressing this idea of strength and force were used in some lace designs in company with the two doves above them, thus symbolising the harmony possible between gentleness, humility and power (figure 130).

127 Border of lacis, late sixteenth century (Victoria and Albert Museum, ref. 32280, London)

128 *Winged heraldic beast*

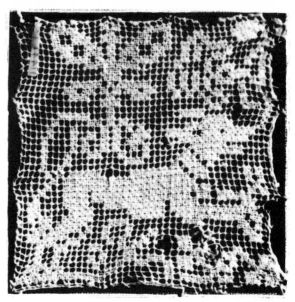

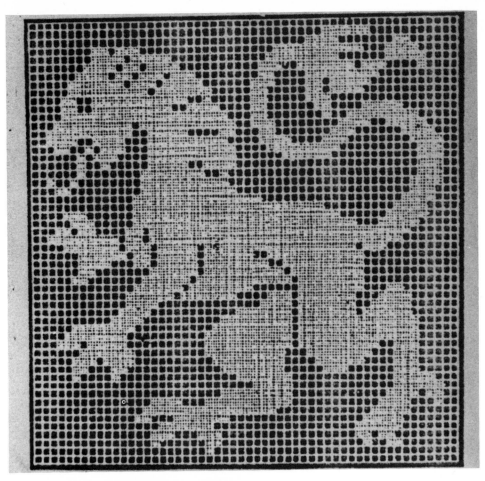

129 Lion

130, 131 A dog and the Agnus Dei *designs, probably from a cover, late sixteenth century, Italian (Victoria and Albert Museum, ref. 26192, London)*

Some designs have been included which may not appeal to anyone to attempt to reproduce – the design would often be quite difficult to work out. Yet they help us to share in the atmospheres in which the early lacemakers pondered over their work (see figures 114, 115 and 117).

In their minds would also be other symbolic ideas connected with their designs. Some of these were given by 'Carita' in her book *Lacis*.[35] As the unicorn's horn was considered to be an antidote to poison, so it was often found on a pattern of lacis when used for all objects connected with food. The hart in the depth of the forest suggested solitude as also did the lion, in one aspect of its ways, as well as its strength and sovereignty. The lamb spoke not only of gentleness and innocence, but also of sacrifice, with the well-known device of '*Agnus Dei*' (figure 131). The worldly pride we noticed for the peacock yet also included wisdom; while, with the pelican the phoenix, also spoke of resurrection. The pomegranate's seeds gave hope of immortality. But the dragon represented evil and sin.

Certainly in ecclesiastical productions are to be seen sermons in woven threads.

Was there some special meaning involved when the beasts and birds were so often arranged in groups of two facing each other, with a tree form, or a vase, or shield between them? (figure 130.) One remembers the transformation that occurred to the images of the vase and lily of the Annunciation pictures, as their meaning was lost after years of repetitions. So the separating forms would probably have originated as having a religious significance.

Recently in the Victoria and Albert Museum I noticed a column (dated 1200 AD) where the carving of the capital showed on one side the figure of Daniel, and on another two birds in this 'opposing' position. Below those birds were two other, smaller ones, not facing but retreating from each other. That happens also in lace designs (figure 10).

By what processes of thought or of a differing symbolism did this different grouping develop? In the lace work more frequently birds are found in similar groupings (as seen in the reference to *A Scholehouse for the Needle*).

There is quite a different arrangement of the animals and birds shown in figure 132, which may be suggesting their creation and life in the Garden of Eden. Even serpent-looking creatures are curling their way between the unicorn, ostrich and leopard, while a deer, boar and elephant wander above, among rabbit, owl, monkey, dog, fox and squirrel, with birds of all kinds, including the dove, flying among them. The peaceful scene achieves a certain dignity of movement in the poise of the larger animals and a delightful scattering around of their smaller companions, while the two trees rising centrally lead one up to the fruitful trees above and the birds flying among them. It is a satisfying design.

It is a much more crowded community seen in figure 133. So many creatures are here, great and small, fierce and gentle, yet happily finding room for all, even though definitely crowded. How did the peacock so beautifully arrange his tail?

May I suggest, in leaving the main discussion of the influence of symbolism on the lace designs, that this picture might have been suggested by the passage in Isaiah, chapter X.

The wolf also shall dwell with the lamb, and the leopard shall lie down with the kid: and the calf and the young lion and

*the fatlings together . . . They shall not
hurt nor destroy in all my holy mountain.*

Adapting a symbol for a filet lace
design is an excellent way of learning
the craft, and it is hoped that readers of
this book will enjoy not only following
the charts and illustrations but also be
more ambitious and design and make
larger pieces of filet lace themselves.

*132 Darned netting panel probably repre-
senting The Creation, sixteenth century
(Victoria and Albert Museum, ref.
50206, London)*

Overleaf
*133 Lacis work, seventeenth century,
Italian (Victoria and Albert Museum,
ref. K2470, London)*

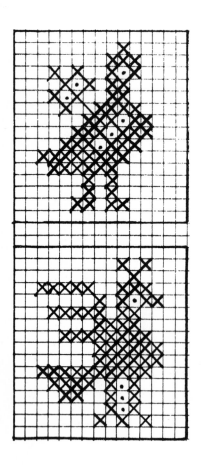

References

1 *Book of Guipure D'Art* – Madame Goubard, Ward Lock, London, 1869
2 *Encyclopedia of Needlework* – Thérèse de Dillmont, DMC
3 Miss Elizabeth Dennis in *Embroidery* 1961
4 *Lacis*, 'Carita' (Mrs I. A. Simpson) Sampson Low, London, 1908
5 *Seven Centuries of Lace*, Mrs Hungerford Pollen, Heinemann, London, 1908
6 *The Art of Embroidery*, Marie Schuette and Sigrid Müller-Christensen, Thames and Hudson, London
7 *Renaissance Patterns for Lace and Embroidery* – Federico Vinciolo 1587, facsimile reprint, Dover Publications, New York, 1971
8 *History of Lace* – Mrs Bury Palliser, Sampson Low, London, 1901
9 *Lacis* – 'Carita' (Mrs I. A. Simpson) 1908
10 *History of Lace* – Mrs Bury Palliser, Sampson Low, London, 1908
11 *Pillow Lace* – Elizabeth Mincoff and Margaret Marriage, John Murray, London, 1907
12 *Hand-made Bobbin Lace Work*, Margaret Maidment, Branford, 1954 reprint, Mass. USA
13 *Pillow Lace*, E. Mincoff and M. Marriage, John Murray, London, 1907
14 *Seven Centuries of Lace*, Mrs Hungerford Pollen, Heinemann, London, 1908
15 *Lace*, Virginia Churchill Bath, Cassell and Collier, London, 1974
16 *Lacis*, 'Carita' (Mrs I. A. Simpson), Sampson Low, London, 1908
17 *The Needlework of Mary Queen of Scots*, Van Nostrand Reinhold, New York, 1973
18 *Handbook of Designs and Devices*, Clarence P. Horning, Dover Publications, New York
19 *Seven Centuries of Lace*, Mrs Hungerford Pollen, Heinemann, London, 1908
20 *Samplers*, Averil Colby, Batsford, London, 1964
21 *Seven Centuries of Lace*, Mrs Hungerford Pollen, Heinemann, London, 1908
22 *The Art of Embroidery*, Marie Schuette and Sigrid Müller-Christensen, Thames and Hudson, London, 1964
23 *Samplers*, Averil Colby, Batsford, London, 1964
24 *The Art of Embroidery*, Marie Schuette and Sigrid Müller-Christensen, Thames and Hudson, London, 1964
25 *The Aegean Civilisation*, Gustave Glotz, Routledge and Kegan Paul, London, 1976
26 *Seven Centuries of Lace*, Mrs Hungerford Pollen, Heinemann, London, 1908
27 *The Art of Embroidery*, Marie Schuette and Sigrid Müller-Christensen, Thames and Hudson, London, 1964
28 *English Historical Embroidery*, Barbara Snook, Batsford, London, 1960: Mills and Boon, 1974
29 *Pillow Lace*, Mincoff and Marriage, Murray, London, 1907, reprint 1972
30 *The Art of Embroidery*, Marie Schuette and Sigrid Müller-Christensen, Thames and Hudson, London, 1964
31 Walter De La Mare, 'All That's Past'
32 *Renaissance Patterns For Lace And Embroidery*, Federico Vinciolo 1587, Facsimile. Dover Publications, New York, 1971
33 *A Scholehouse For The Needle*, Richard Shoreleyker, London, 1625
34 *The Etruscans*, Werner Keller, Jonathan Cape, London, 1975
35 *Lacis*, 'Carita' (Mrs I. A. Simpson), Sampson Low, London, 1908

Bibliography

Bath, Virginia Churchill, *Lace*, Cassell and Collier Macmillan, London, 1974

Bocher, Emmanuel, *Manuel Des Travaux a l'Aiguille – Le Filet Brodé*, Paris, 1911

Boucherit, Edouard, *Grand Album de Models pour Filet*, Paris

Boucherit, Edouard, *Le Filet Brodé*, Paul Dupont, Paris

Colby, Averil, *Samplers*, Batsford, London, 1964

Dillmont, Therese de, *Encyclopaedia of Needlework*, D M C, 1891

Encyclopaedia of Victorian Needlework, Dover Publications, 1972 (facsimile copy of *A Dictionary of Needlework*)

Fischbach, Frederick, *Lace Album Designs for Lace*, privately printed, St Gall, Switzerland, 1878

Glotz, Gustave, *The Aegean Civilisation*, Routledge and Kegan Paul, London, 1976

Goubard, Madame, *Book of Guipure D'Art*, Ward Lock, London, 1869

Groves, Sylvia, *The History of Needlework Tools*, Country Life, London, 1966

Horning, C P, *Handbook of Designs and Devices*, Dover Publications, New York, 1959

Jackson, F Nevill, *A History of Hand-made Lace*, L. Upcott Gill, 1900

Jourdain, M *Old Lace – A Handbook for Collectors*, Batsford, London, 1908

Keller, Werner, *The Etruscans*, Jonathan Cape, London, 1975

Maidment, Margaret, *Hand-made Bobbin Lace*, reprint, Branford, Boston, USA, 1954

Mague, Charles, *Les Dentelles Anciennes*, Les Editions Pittoresques, Paris, 1930

Melen, Lisa, *Knotting and Netting*, Van Nostrand Reinhold, New York, 1972

Mincoff, E and Marriage, M, *Pillow Lace*, John Murray, London, 1907, Reprint 1972

Palliser, E Bury, *The History of Lace*, Sampson Low, London, 1901

Pollen, Mrs John Hungerford, *Seven Centuries of Lace*, Heinemann, London, 1908

Schuette, Marie and Christensen, Sigrid Müller, *The Art of Embroidery*, Thames and Hudson, London, 1964

Simpson, I A, Mrs, 'Carita', *Lacis Filet Brodé*, Sampson Low, London, 1910

Snook, Barbara, *English Historical Embroidery*, Batsford, 1960: Mills & Boon, London, 1970

Swain, Margaret, *The Needlework of Mary Queen of Scots*, Van Nostrand Reinhold, New York

Tolkien, J R R, editor–The Early English Text of the *Ancrene Riwle (Ancrene Wisse)*, Oxford University Press, 1967

Vinciolo, Federico, *Renaissance Patterns for Lace & Embroidery*, 1587, facsimile reproduction, Dover Publications, 1971

Wolf & Dupayron, *Le Filet Ancien*, Several Volumes, Wolf & Dupayron, Paris

Needlecraft Monthly magazine 1908

Suppliers

Threads and machine-made filet net
Cuyahoga Studio
Joanne Graham
17a Hastings Road
Bexhill-on-Sea, East Sussex

de Denne Limited
159–161 Kenton Road
Harrow
Middlesex
For threads

A Sells
Lane Cove
49 Pedley Lane
Clifton,
Shefford,
Bedfordshire

Netting needles in steel and ivory
Netting meshes from 3 mm ($\frac{1}{8}$ in.)
Wire frames from 127 mm (5 in.) square
These are made to order by
Theodore Fabergé
30 Downs Road
Hastings
East Sussex

Mountings
M & M Marketing & Management Services
183 Grestone Avenue
Handsworth Wood
Birmingham B20 1NA
For picture frames, paperweights, etc

Daphne Gulliver
30 Darnell Drive
Chesham, Bucks

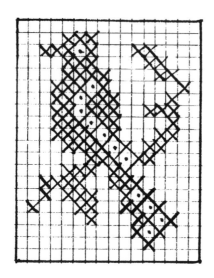

Index